EGOTOPIA

EGOTOPIA

NARCISSISM AND

THE NEW AMERICAN

LANDSCAPE

John Miller

With a Foreword by Ashley Montagu

The University of Alabama Press
Tuscaloosa and London

Copyright © 1997
The University of Alabama Press
Tuscaloosa, Alabama 35487-0380
All rights reserved
Manufactured in the United States of America

∞

The paper on which this book is printed meets the
minimum requirements of American National Standard
for Information Science-Permanence of Paper for
Printed Library Materials, ANSI Z39.48-1984.

Library of Congress Cataloging-in-Publication Data

Miller, John, 1946 Mar. 11–
      Egotopia : narcissism and the new American landscape / John Miller ;
with a foreword by Ashley Montagu.
          p.   cm.
      Includes index.
      ISBN 0-8173-0901-2 (cloth : alk. paper)
      1. Landscape—United States—History—20th century.
2. Aesthetics, American—History—20th century.   3. Landscape—
Unites States—Psychological aspects—History—20th century.
4. Narcissism—Social aspects—United States—History—20th century.
5. Unites States—Civilization—1970–   I. Title.
BH301.L3M55   1997
304.2′3′0973—dc21   97-10770

British Library Cataloguing-in-Publication Data available

The illustrations on the first half-title and title pages are from a photograph
of billboards dominating the landscape, courtesty of Scenic America.

In memory of Dr. and Mrs. Norbert Fuerst

CONTENTS

FOREWORD

I completed reading John Miller's *Egotopia,* as Shelley once said upon finishing a book, "in a frenzy of enthusiasm." *Egotopia* is a marvelous book, and nothing could be more timely. Emerson and Thoreau would have rejoiced in it, as would a good many of our other celebrated culture heroes. Whether through the novel, essay, poetry, play, philosophy, or more specialized work, like Rachel Carson's *Silent Spring,* these writers, though severe critics of the United States, all loved their country, and in their own concerned critical ways fully endorsed Scott Fitzgerald's moving words, "America is a willingness of the heart."

This willingness of the heart, this American generosity, especially through private gifts, has enriched our colleges and universities and made our museums of art and sciences among the greatest and most beautiful in the world. The United States, somewhat late in getting started, has gradually become the world's center for the arts, a center of such virtuosity that it attracts many talents from the rest of the world. This willingness of the heart is a reflection of the American spirit that Europeans frequently remark when they visit the United States and that is extended to the whole world. But danger from extremists on the right as well as those on the left threaten the American aesthetic sense. Some two hundred years ago William Blake wrote, "Degrade first the arts if you'd mankind degrade." In the twentieth century, Hitler, the product of a highly civilized Austria, well understood Blake's sentiment, as have some members of Congress.

Miller examines the dark side of the American character, the side that with rare acumen and skill he critically dissects. I know of no book that more effectively enables us to understand America's growing disregard of aesthetics and the nature of the psychosis from which our country suffers than *Egotopia*.

Miller's examination of the United States in the last decade of the twentieth century is devastating, and like the good physician, having diagnosed the disease and its causes, he does not fail to prescribe the cure. He makes brilliantly clear that the egotistical embrace of private sensibilities in the new American landscape, the narcissistic self-indulging that has replaced the self-transcendence of earlier days, is illuminated by the ubiquity of, indeed, the legitimization and institutionalization of, the "quick fix," namely, psychotherapy. In the anomic world in which people have grown out of touch with one another, such therapy, Miller shows, serves as a principal mechanism for the transformation of public into private values and the development of the New Man. The result has been the emergence of the megaself, a perverted individualism negating moral, ethical, and religious constraints on individual behavior.

Miller writes incisively on the ugliness of our consumer society, anatomizing in detail the inner ugliness of egotopia, the debilitating defect of collective character that has the capacity of ultimately destroying the last vestiges of aesthetic consciousness and civility. Our own worst selves, set loose and unrestrained, may yet put an end to a creature and a culture that once held such high promise. No one has ever made this more clear than Miller in this magnificent call to action.

In 1920 with the publication, the achievement, of his monumental *Outline of History,* H. G. Wells concluded that "history is a race between education and catastrophe." I read the book in 1922, and that phrase has stayed with me ever since, for it was not only illuminating but also prophetic. Sad to say in his last book, *Mind at the End of its Tether,* published in 1945, less than a year before his death, Wells was deeply pessimistic about the future of humankind. He had understood clearly what a critical role education plays in enabling people to think and to take an active part in the government of their community and their country. The first requisite is the ability to think, and in the Western world that ability has been strongly discouraged by the kind of "education" to which its victims have been subjected. From first to last our schools teach their students *what* to think rather than *how* to think. The result from every point of view has been disastrous, for it leads to the death of education and inevitably to its makeshift, *instruction,* the technologization of education. Under such conditions the "how" and "what" are conflated, leading to the inability to separate the one from the other, with the consequent reign of confusion in which words become stereotypes with unexamined presuppositions and the icons of reality. It is a dangerous situation ready for any ideologue to take advantage of.

What then should education be? Originally the word *education,* derived from the Latin *educare,* meant to care for, to nourish, and to cause to grow. And what does one mean by healthy growth and development? First and foremost, the need to love, to work, to play, and to think, to use one's mind critically. As we are today, we can hardly be said to understand the real meaning of those words. We have for many years now been flattering ourselves that we can make machines that think like human beings, failing to recognize, especially in this frantic cybernetic age, that we have increasingly and efficiently been making human beings who think like machines. This, too, we hope shall pass, but unless we are careful, it may not, and we shall all end up like robots happy in the technological blessings that have brought us to such a state of bliss.

Though he does not deal at length with education, Miller has much to say along these lines. The present American landscape, which is "ultimately a manifestation of the inner chaos that defines the New Man—rampant ego, blatant narcissistic self-indulgence," he would replace with an alternative landscape, an American public landscape defined not by market forces, but by "public and communal values even if its function were entirely and exclusively commercial." "Ultimately," Miller says, "the value of the public landscape would be precisely in proportion to its noncommercial appearance and visual character."

Essentially, Miller's chief concern throughout the book is how we in the United States will choose to live in the next century. In that connection Miller raises many significant questions that cry out for answers, each of which is derivative from the central question: How did we get to be the way we are now? Miller in his beautiful prose has with great clarity set out the answer to that challenging question.

Foreword

Egotopia is a magnificent and vitally important book, and like the true meaning of a word, namely, the action it produces, its message we hope will be carried wide and far and will prevail.

ASHLEY MONTAGU

ACKNOWLEDGMENTS

F ew first-time authors are so fortunate as to attract the attention and receive the endorsement of Ashley Montagu, one of the most eminent and respected critics of contemporary American culture. Dr. Montagu's enthusiasm in writing a foreword to *Egotopia* is a genuine testimony to the critical need for increased understanding of the New American Landscape and the rapidly emerging American megaself. The rise of narcissism, the transformation of public into private values, and the subsequent aesthetic degradation of the environment pose serious questions about identity, values, and aesthetics on the eve of a new millennium. We should all be grateful for Ashley Montagu's support in focusing public attention on these issues.

I am particularly appreciative of the many contributions to *Egotopia* made by Edward McMahon, a founder and past president of Washington, D.C.–based Scenic America and director of the American Greenways Program at the Conservation Fund in Arlington, Virginia. I am especially indebted for his help with the chapter on billboards, although I take full responsibility for the conclusions therein concerning Scenic America. No one has been more dedicated to improving the aesthetics of the American environment than Ed McMahon. Those of us concerned with preserving and enhancing the urban and rural landscape owe him our gratitude for his life-long commitment to taming the aesthetic excesses of mindless commercialism.

During the course of completing *Egotopia*, few friends have been as steadfast in their encouragement and as constant a source of inspiration as Robert Leonard Reid. Conservationist, mountain climber, dedicated outdoorsman, editor of *A Treasury of the Sierra Nevada,* and author of *Mountains of the Great Blue Dream*—Reid's writing and life reflect the moral and physical high ground to which he has always aspired. I am pleased to be among those who can say they have been with Reid in the Sierra.

Egotopia would not be a reality without the continued and enthusiastic support of Hal Lockwood of Penmarin Books. His suggestions regarding revisions to the original manuscript were of the greatest value. I am particularly indebted to him for his wise counsel regarding the perplexing and challenging task of finding an appropriate publisher.

I wish to thank the following individuals for reviewing the manuscript and offering helpful suggestions: Dr. Virginia Vertiz, Stephanie Schubert, Anne Knight, J. Peter Nelson, and of course Curtis L. Clark, senior editor at The University of Alabama Press. Special thanks to Frank Vespe, director of policy at Scenic America, for locating and granting permission to use the photograph on the title page.

Acknowledgments

EGOTOPIA

1 DARK SATANIC MALLS

For William Blake, the nineteenth-century English poet and social critic, the industrial revolution was more than an assault on agrarian sensibility and tradition. Blake understood that the forces of industrialization and the continued concentration of population in the burgeoning urban centers spelled the end of an economy and a culture defined by man's intimate association with nature.

For Blake, a most disturbing casualty of the industrial revolution was the demise of beauty. Machinery and the brute forces of production deflowered the tender and vulnerable aesthetics of England's green and pleasant land. In his poem "Milton," Blake warned of dark satanic mills. Images of a satanically inspired industrial ugliness choking the landscape in coal dust and chimney soot decried the factory's ascendancy over the farm. The aesthetics of an agrarian society were literally transformed into the industrial ugliness of the shop floor, the factory yard, the dock, the mine, the mill.

One hundred and seventy years after Blake's death, the lost aesthetics of the pre-industrial agrarian epoch continue to attract and entice—subconsciously, subtly, yet persistently. The aesthetics of that pre-industrial agrarian epoch continue to appeal to an unidentified and unacknowledged, but no less insatiable, appetite for beauty. Our less-than-conscious infatuation with the pre-industrial agrarian past is, at some fundamental level, a yearning for the aesthetics of paradise lost.

Of course, as both Dante and John Milton, two poets intimately associated with concepts of paradise, would attest, paradise is not paradise without the presence of man. Beauty encompasses far more than an undisturbed natural landscape. Beauty can also be the result of a particularly felicitous juxtaposition of man's endeavors, sensitive and respectful of the prerogatives of nature. Such enriched unions of civilization and landscape are possible, if improbable, even in an urban and otherwise aesthetically oppressive environment.

However, we possess no conscious desire to experience, nor to become proponents of, these almost magical landscapes in which man and nature create aesthetic impressions greater than the sum total of their component parts. Like some Platonic ideal, or Kantian noumena, these rare and unique couplings of man and nature seem incapable of being identified and experienced. They occur with greater frequency within the hazy realms of imagination than in the Monday mornings of a suburban rush-hour reality.

Since the demise of the agrarian epoch, these magical landscapes have become blurred and unreliable images, elusive fancies, fleeting ethereal notions, flickering racial memories. Although the impulse to seek out and celebrate such aesthetically pleasing locales must undoubtedly whisper and cajole, such whispers incite no conscious awareness of a hunger for the aesthetics of the agrarian zeitgeist. No, we are not infatuated with the pre-industrial Eden in conscious rejection of the aesthetics of modernity. Our romantic idealization of the lost agrarian landscape animates, informs, and distorts a peculiar American attempt, not to reclaim a lost aesthetic, but to recapture the harmonious balance between man and his physical environment.

Interdependence. Man-in-nature. Nature-in-man. Such abstractions give rise to both environmental, back-to-the-land ecofantasies and equally fantastic imagery of rugged individualists on the frontier. Whither go aesthetics amidst these contemporary stylized agrarian myths?

Displeasure with the contemporary landscape is subconscious, undefined, and seldom considered an aesthetic issue. We are reluctant to consciously acknowledge a discontent whose origins are aesthetic. We are not accustomed to understanding ourselves aesthetically. We have failed to properly acknowledge, identify, and chronicle the uncomely and vexatious aesthetics of either the passing industrial or the postindustrial age.

Historically, we have chosen to define ourselves in terms of the utility, not the aesthetics, of physical space: the farm, the small town, the city, the great suburban diaspora. The utility of these physical spaces provides answers to questions of identity. Having no apparent utility—or considered a negation of utility—the aesthetics of physical space in twentieth-century America are of no value as a source of identity. Aesthetics remains a nonissue.

Now, on the threshold of cyberspace, the concept of utility itself is extended to electronically created space. That being the case, the information age shares with its industrial precursor no aesthetic value. As time passes and the agrarian epoch becomes ever more a historical abstraction, the concept of aesthetics becomes increasingly problematic to the American consciousness. We have neither understood nor appreciated Blake's realization that that which dominates a society defines its sense of aesthetics. The farm dominated nineteenth-century America just as the factory dominated much of the twentieth century. Today, both the landscape and the consciousness of America are not so much dominated as culturally trivialized by the ubiquitous shopping mall.

Despite a thorough analysis by cultural critics and talk show pundits, the fundamental significance of the shopping mall has been overlooked. The shopping mall is much more than a culmination of careless suburban planning and overzealous commercial excess. It is a harbinger of a soon-to-be-realized future aesthetic that will devastate our contemporary landscape even more than the factory dominated and eventually eclipsed the appealing ambiance of the farm. The shopping mall is not the end of a declining American aesthetic. It is only the beginning of an increasingly precipitous decline. For all their gaudy tinsel and bright illumination, these temples of consumption impart a metaphorical darkness, which Blake, were he with us today, most certainly would identify as a foreboding aesthetic, a dark satanic mall.

To understand the changing American landscape is to understand it aesthetically. An aesthetic interpretation of the landscape is not peripheral but central to understanding the physical transformation of post-industrial society. The failure to understand, acknowledge, and explain the fundamental significance of rapid and dramatic change, in both private and public physical spaces, has been a failure to interpret such change aesthetically. Without an aesthetic interpretation, history, demographics, sociology, and architecture offer merely discrete, patternless, and essentially incomplete and unsatisfying explanations of the transition from farm, to factory, to shopping mall, and beyond.

To grasp fully the dynamics of the changing American landscape is to identify and ultimately understand an emerging twenty-first-century American aesthetic. While being neither as benign as the agrarian nor as de facto as the industrial, the New American Landscape will be the first synthetic environment in history whose aesthetics will systematically anesthetize those who call it home. We cannot afford to misinterpret the portents of things to come.

To understand how and why the American landscape is changing it is necessary to understand how and why we have become a nation of suburban mishmash. The suburbs encircle historic city centers. They sweep outward into what is left of the countryside. They are dominated by shopping malls— the contemporary commercial equivalent of the medieval castle—that impose an economic and cultural hegemony on the immediate neighborhood.

The suburbanization of America has not been solely a result of simple economic growth. Neither is it entirely a function of race and social factors. Rather, suburbanization encompasses an aesthetic appeal that emerged in the demise of the ideal of the city. America has become suburbanized because the idea and the ideal of the city failed, broke down, to be replaced by the idea and the ideal of the suburb. The contemporary and future American landscape can only be fully understood within the context of changing notions of individual and collective identity.

At the end of the Second World War, with industrial pro-

duction at full throttle, horizons of soot-belching smoke-
stacks cast an appalling ugliness over scores of cities throughout the nation. The depression and the war motivated hundreds of thousands to leave farms and small towns for
industrial jobs in the big cities. The city was the portal
through which the poor came, from the country and from
abroad. Their desire for work, schooling, and opportunities infused the city with the passions we once considered
progress.

It was in the city that we sensed something being built, an
enterprise under construction—not just for the fortunate few
but in some meaningful sense for everyone. The city was
growing up, and those in the city were growing up with
it, taking on responsibilities while thinking they were big
enough and smart enough to get the job done. Many believed
that the city was open to those committed to a vision of collective responsibility. Historically, the city existed as a common ground for the mutual benefit of all. Even the lowly but
dignified workingman was not just a member of a clan but a
citizen of that body that transcends the clan, defined by, and
imbued with, a *Pax Urbana.*

Many shared such a spirit as the twentieth-century American city prospered. Postwar economic growth enabled thousands to escape its industry and blue-collar neighborhoods
for the wide-open spaces of the working-class suburbs. Factory workers symbolically reconnected themselves to their
rural roots. For them, the overnight miracle of the newly built
suburb was a symbol of the authentically pastoral.

Where corn fields had recently stood, grassy building plots
60 feet wide by 120 feet deep beckoned the working class to

come home to the land. The great suburban transformation beginning after the war was fueled by the unarticulated but real notion that every family, even working-class families, deserved to escape from the aesthetics of the factory. Their reward was a piece of America the Beautiful.

However, no one in my family said we were moving to the suburbs to escape the ugly steel mill neighborhood of Cleveland, Ohio, where I was born. In the 1950s and 1960s, after years of factory work, my father and his friends did not suddenly develop a sense of aesthetics, nor a desire to re-create their youth on the farm. No, they, and countless others, prosperous from labor union–negotiated wages, were turning their backs on the city and becoming suburbanites. Beauty had nothing to do with it. Fear had everything to do with it.

My father would not share the city with people unlike himself. The concept of a city big and broad enough to encompass every race and class required an imagination and a faith beyond his capability. For those like him, a symbolic wedge split city from suburb, dividing society as decisively as did the designations "town" and "country."

By the 1970s, for many the American city was dead, or certainly dying. My father could not understand that he was a principal agent in the very decline of the city he had so cherished. The decline of the American city is the story of abandonment. My father abandoned the great American myth of the open city, the democratic city, the cosmopolitan city, the city that appealed to our better natures.

From the 1960s through the 1990s, the American city has been redefined. Both the city's opponents and proponents agree that the myth of inclusivity and community values is more myth than reality. Consider the implications of a fragmented and adversarial urban America so aptly chronicled each day by our tireless media:

— The American city is inhabited by increasing numbers of people who are destructive of the very city on which they are economically dependent. At best, such people appear to be unable fiscally, physically, or spiritually to assist in its maintenance or reconstruction.

— The American city is each day occupied by an invasion of nonresident employees who do not dwell within its jurisdiction. They appropriate what remains of the city's economic and cultural resources while denying any responsibility or obligation to its welfare.

— The American city is the prime venue for increasingly lucrative criminal enterprises, especially drugs, whose sale results in random and senseless acts of violence and contributes to the further spread of AIDS.

— The American city is home to the most expensive yet least effective primary and secondary education systems in our history, responsible for generations of illiterates, better prepared for the nineteenth than the twenty-first century.

— The American city is economically enfeebled and, in seeking another financial fix from the federal government, has assumed the role of either beggar or bully.

— The American city, after years of heightened environmental concern, continues to endure bad air, bad water, noise pollution, and the congestion of automobiles.

The conditions that describe the plight of our cities, to an increasing extent, also describe our suburbs. After fifty years of trying to separate itself physically and psychologically from the city on which it economically and socially depends, the American suburb has succumbed to many of the same afflictions as the city itself.

The suburbs did not free Americans from the ugliness of the industrial city at mid-century. Beautiful outlying development envisioned by the proponents of suburban expansion in the late 1940s and early 1950s did not materialize. Instead, the suburbs have recast and redefined ugliness in the form of tract housing, commercial strip development, and, of course, the ubiquitous high art of the regional shopping mall.

Yes, there may be real and imagined differences between the ugliness of the inner city and the suburban fringe. Nonetheless, aesthetically, the city and the suburb became increasingly indivisible in a joint collaboration to negate aesthetics in favor of utility. The fluid interdependency and indivisibility of urban and suburban America mock the artificial and often meaningless distinctions between city and suburb.

City. Suburb. Countryside. To travel across America, to live in much of the nation, is to experience a landscape that is truly indivisible. Whatever we choose to call it, its commonalities often surpass its differences. Both the city and its suburbs seem to exhibit a moral malaise. The metaphor of sickness and ill health is routinely employed to characterize the pathology by which urban and suburban America is debilitated. Consider the metaphor—not of ill health but of death itself—to most accurately describe the reality of the American city and its indivisible suburban and exurban manifestations.

Yet, of course, the American city is not dead. It still exists and so too do we. We still function, we still exert our individual and collective wills in a vain attempt to impose ourselves on the cosmos. We still make money, make love,

Dark Satanic Malls

and some of us make a name for ourselves, whether it be on the street corners of the ghetto or in corner offices of other, better-known streets. However, does all of this mean that the city yet lives?

One is intrigued by the notion that the city neither lives nor dies. Rather, the city is in some kind of perpetual resurrection of itself, willing its rebirth, only to die again because the conditions necessary for the city to truly live do not exist. We have come to expect our cities to be unlikable, unhealthy, and unlivable, to possess all the characteristics of social, cultural, fiscal, and physical death. But like a vampire, the American city continues to function—undead, in some permanent pathological imitation of life. Like a vampire, the city is sustained only by the substance of those it assimilates.

I did not realize until years afterward that my father, even in his suburban incarnation, was among the first of the city's victims. He became an undead inhabitant of the great undead city, rejecting a public consciousness as is characteristic of the transition from public to private man. His was the undeath of a glassy-eyed stare, of peering into the street from behind a curtained window. His connection to others he experienced by watching the local TV news. My father's private world was a crude and unfashionable precursor of today's contemporary undeath, which completely substitutes individual private interests for collective public concerns. The pursuit and attainment of material acquisitions and psychotherapeutic validation are bereft of democratic and public values. Not surprisingly, they are tailored to an age in which the private interests of private men are of primary concern.

It is essential to understand that in the context of a post-industrial consumer economy the private interests of private men are essentially commercial and materialistic. Private man does not turn his back on society, is not the 1960s drop out, not even the traditional aristocrat who finds commercial trade distasteful. We should not confuse private man with the legendary American individual. Individualism loses its social utility and its normative meaning when public concern no longer informs individual character. The private man pursuing private ends offers us little more than an exercise in self-interest.

The death of the city is the death of public man, for it is in the city that public man truly comes to life. The death of the city is the death of the facility for social understanding by which public man defined and comprehended the public realm. From the interaction and ultimately the mutual tolerance of competing interests, classes, races, and clans came a rich tapestry of social custom. Such traditions impose a public sense of order and identity on chaos.

The myth and the reality of the American city were a living testament to, and social manifestation of, the life process, ever struggling yet never succeeding in defining our identity. The city became the mechanism whereby singly and collectively, psychologically and sociologically, we struggled to construct our individual and corporate selves. Of course, the job of construction was not to be completed, nor to be finished, for life's journey, not life's destination, was the reward.

Public man instinctively understood the inherent value to individuals and institutions of the process of becoming, of journeying toward a destination that will never be reached. The city of public men pursuing public ends in the public realm defined our ultimate concern. The city demonstrated that our private foibles, weaknesses, and failures are insignificant compared to the accomplishment of our larger and mutually inclusive public enterprise.

However, the death of the city and the swelling of the ranks of the undead signifies our disavowal of journeying toward a destination that is never to be reached. No longer are we to be satisfied by what we consider the dubious rewards of merely striving to construct our individual and corporate selves. Today, we believe in the power of our technology to literally achieve individual and collective ends. We have faith in technology to accomplish what faith in the nontechnical was apparently unable to achieve. This faith in the perfectibility of technology is really a faith in our own perfectibility, for our technology is, of course, a product and an extension of ourselves. In believing in the perfectibility of our technology, we banish from the city what had been its most human quality: the individual and collective understanding and acceptance of our imperfect but persistent will. We have rejected the inevitability of human imperfection because we no longer believe human imperfection to be more than a temporary impediment. Unwilling to accept our imperfect will, we believe in a perfectible private personality. In abandoning the public acknowledgment and acceptance of our imperfect will, we have publicly endorsed the private fulfillment of our individual desires.

The death of the city, and its reoccurring resurrection, is the obsession with achieving self-perfection. In trying to achieve self-perfection we fail to realize perfection is only an illusion, not a reality. In our obsession with self-perfection, we deny history, for history informs us of our imperfections.

Dark Satanic Malls

The death of the city is the triumph of our belief in perfection as much as it is the end of history. The death of the city is the triumph of technique over life. It is the technical mastery of imitating life in the absence of life. We have substituted the will to perfection for the will to live. The city persists, at once both a vampire and a robot, virtually sustained by the blood of its victims, yet ironically graceless, mechanical, inhuman. All is technique.

If the city is dead, what of the countryside? While at some fundamental level we have come to accept the death of the city, we have not acknowledged the death of the American countryside. Unlike the city, the death of the countryside is not immediately apparent to us. The death of the countryside does not create dysfunction, disruption, trauma, and recurring pathology. The death of the countryside has been perceived, if perceived at all, as more a gradual diminution of its unique physical, psychic, mystical, and metaphorical identity. Yet the countryside has become urban without becoming a true city, in whatever the best sense of the word *city* still signifies. As the city's physical character becomes more intensely urban, we witness the urbanization of what had once been truly rural.

Fifty years ago we were a nation of well-defined, -bounded, and -bordered cities, separated from self-contained small towns by rural areas. Today we are a nation in which the boundaries between city and country, rural area and small town, have been continuously eroded. In much of the United States the inner city is surrounded by layers of suburbs. Regional new towns exist along interstates and adjacent to the original urban core. In many areas the term *countryside* is more historic than real, and it no longer makes sense to speak of city, town, and countryside, for such descriptive categories have no corresponding physical reality.

The death of the American countryside has exhausted the wellspring of American values. As the writer Wallace Stegner pointed out, in wilderness is the salvation of the world. From our collective pastoral experience came the notion of public man, perhaps best defined as a moral compromise and social balance between individual and communal interests. The concept of public man imbued the national character with a sense of equity and justice. It is no surprise that in American mythology we return to the redemptive countryside to set straight our moral compass.

The city, with its diverse and competing populations, posed an inherent risk to the moral compromise and social balance between individual and community established on the American frontier. Only by urbanizing the mythology of public man, in pursuit of public ends, can the whole of the city become greater than its individual competing parts. Only then can the reality of the city supplement and enrich an American character so greatly defined by our experience of the land.

The greatness of the city has been its cosmopolitan tolerance of diversity, its cultural achievement, its ability to engender urbanity and civility itself. Ironically and paradoxically, this urban achievement has always been dependent on the continued existence of the countryside and its tradition-bound small towns. Our concept of public man has been refined and improved upon in the city. However, we must not forget that public man was born of the American pastoral experience, an experience whose continued unique identity serves to enrich and sustain all the city has accomplished.

Dark Satanic Malls

Consider the often dismal and stifling small-mindedness that is the classic failure of the rural sensibility. The irrepressible American will strives to bend the small town's constricting bonds of conformity but not to break its nurturing fellowship. In forging the city from the diverse multitudes, that same imperfect yet persistent American will becomes fully conscious of its inability to bend the city into a desired shape without breaking the city into pieces. Only in and through the mitigating mediation of public man can the city be forged, bending but not breaking in the process.

The notion of the urban public realm is an analog to the organic and seasonal character of the countryside. In this version of the urban incarnation, the city as an organic public enterprise is the urban equivalent of our experience on the land. For the city to flower, its roots in the countryside cannot be destroyed. For the city to flower, those qualities that make the countryside uniquely pastoral cannot be sacrificed.

The American countryside's very essence was its welcome retreat from urban hegemony and, paradoxically, its regrettable distance and isolation from the city's seductive temptations. The countryside of American folklore calls to us today precisely because we continue to understand it as a realm of the imagination, of romantic illusion, of charming and naive innocence. Regrettably, we revere only a fading memory, a ghostly presence of our rural past. The American countryside is no longer innocent because it is no longer isolated. We have architecturally, economically, and culturally connected much of the once physically isolated countryside to urban America by the indisputable umbilical cord of commercial development.

We have arrived at the point in history at which a traveler

Dark Satanic Malls

in the "country" is at no comparative disadvantage to an urban visitor. In city and country alike we may partake of fast food, a night's lodging, or a burst of spontaneous shopping. Much of the countryside is now a mere imitation of the city, an urban rural coupling that combines the worst of both worlds.

The death of the city is inexorably linked to the death of the countryside, and their demise has permitted the creation and the establishment of the New American Landscape. Much of the New American Landscape has been inherited from the old American landscape. Hideous elevated signs trumpet the presence of fast food outlets and discount gas stations along what were once pleasant winding roads meandering through countrified residential neighborhoods.

Multistoried, multifaced billboards with flashing lights and extended and moving parts tower above elementary schools, loom near hospitals, despoil pedestrian walkways, shadow the beach. They are even visible from within the supposedly protected confines of parks, cemeteries, and historic districts. Main streets, once stately and graceful thoroughfares, are blighted by grotesque advertisements, flashing portable signs, intrusive sidewalk placards, and bus benches promoting hair salons and used car lots. Commercial retail establishments dominate the horizon, subordinating residential dwellings in a perpetual state of subservience to the temples of consumption. Aesthetically bleak and morally bankrupt environments are typical in such once diverse places as Los Angeles and Miami, Boston and Seattle.

What is new on the New American Landscape? Unlike the old landscape, the New American Landscape is not merely a physical reality but the manifestation of a dramatic disestab-

Dark Satanic Malls

lishment of public man and a total enshrinement of his private alter ego. Unlike the former countryside, the New American Landscape is not natural. Unlike the former city, it is not historical. The New American Landscape does not just dominate the natural environment; it obliterates the natural environment, just as it obliterates historical experience.

No matter where we live, the New American Landscape establishes for us a national identity that eclipses local or regional distinctiveness. It informs us of our national citizenship in a society committed to advanced and accelerated levels of consumption. The New American Landscape is not incidental, nor accidental, but intentional. For the first time in history the landscape has been designed to stimulate and orchestrate the aggregate consumption of goods and services to facilitate the private pursuit of our individual desires.

What is the primary characteristic of the New American Landscape? I am tempted to say it is unapologetic commercialism and total dedication to utility. The New American Landscape is inherently biased in favor of facilitating consumption. Whatever is perceived as commercially expedient usually triumphs with little regard for the aesthetic cost. More fundamental is its substitution of sensation in place of historical experience as a source of normative values. Once disconnected from the constraints and obligations of history, the landscape becomes the obvious location for enactments and re-enactments of consumer fantasies. The erection of shopping malls and regional theme parks that often appropriate names of historic places while obliterating their history both placate and feed our appetite for novelty and sensation.

Most significantly, the New American Landscape is so disconnected from nature and history that it is essentially plastic in its potential to be created and re-created anew. Plasticity is the fundamental element necessary to facilitate novelty and sensation on the New American Landscape. Maintaining and enhancing this landscape of ahistorical fantasy, and increasing its visual sensation, become a measure of our well-being.

Ironically, an undeniable quality of the New American Landscape is its anesthetic and soporific character. We do not see our wretched aesthetic condition. We do not perceive our addiction to sensation. As a means of self-protection from sensory overload, we have become desensitized to the aggressive pandering of a landscape of novelty and sensation.

As we become more unconscious of our immediate environment, the New American Landscape compensates for our unintended anesthetization by offering increasingly compelling stimuli to awaken our appetites anew. We are more cleverly and persistently enticed to work, play, and live with no respite from the necessity and obligation to seek perfection through unfettered consumption.

In an environment designed to facilitate the private fulfillment of individual desires, we are limited to two options. The first is a conscious awareness of novelty and sensation. The second is a less-than-conscious anesthetization to the world around us. Neither alternative is conducive to the nurturing of aesthetic sensibilities. Our aesthetic impulses and predilections, such as they may be, have been subordinated to commercial purposes. They are to be valued only in terms of their economic utility.

The transformation of public into private man has hastened the deaths of the countryside and the city. Aesthetics are no longer meaningful as a disinterested sense of the beautiful independent of considerations of utility. Serious and significant change has redefined the character of American life with implications for all post-industrial consumer societies. However, we seem unaware of the meaning of what has transpired.

There are moments in history that divide eras—moments that serve to direct our attention, to inform us of a fundamental shift in collective perception, in professed values. The emergence of the New American Landscape is just such a moment, whose significance, for the most part, has escaped the attention of sociologist, historian, and architectural critic alike.

The New American Landscape has completely and totally altered the aesthetics of America. So little of our historic landscape remains that it is difficult to appreciate our present aesthetic deprivation, having few opportunities for comparison. The emergence of the New American Landscape has been a lesson in the failure of our political system to identify and deal with significant social, cultural, and environmental problems. Let us count the ways.

Why did we assume that millions of individuals could be physically relocated from the urban center to the suburban fringe without aesthetic, environmental, and countless other impacts and costs? Thousands of acres of countryside adjacent to existing cities were transformed into residential and commercial developments, the social, environmental, and aesthetic costs of which we have only begun to appreciate.

Few advocated that the impact of such a colossal transformation of the nation's physical environment and collective lifestyle be thoroughly understood through political debate before irreversible decisions were made. Historically, the sub-

Dark Satanic Malls

urban transformation of America was never perceived or defined as a legitimate political issue deserving of the public's attention. This is especially ironic because for decades federal monies financed explosive growth through subsidies of mortgage payments, the federal interstate system, and water and sewage treatment facilities. Yet there were few federally defined and mandated environmental or aesthetic regulations governing this continuing process.

The emergence of the New American Landscape has been one of the most far-reaching social transformations in history, carried out almost invisibly and without public understanding. The market has created the kind of housing, employment, and consumption choices acceptable to the majority of the public. However, as is usually the case, the public does not know the actual cost of the accompanying social, environmental, and aesthetic impacts.

We as a society have failed to take notice of the aesthetics of the New American Landscape. We have failed to see the truth about our aesthetic condition. We have permitted both the city and the countryside to become ugly monuments to commercialism, materialism, and bad taste. Americans are not educated to see and evaluate their environment aesthetically. Instead, we are encouraged by our pragmatic tradition to see distinct pieces but not contextual wholes. Many are concerned about preserving a historic building threatened with demolition, but few understand that real preservation requires nothing less than preserving the architectural and aesthetic integrity of the entire street. For years, one expected architects, urban planners, and certainly environmentalists to lead the public in a growing awareness of how we have sacrificed our historic and scenic heritage. However, those most likely by virtue of training, sensitivity, and sensibility to make the aesthetics of the New American Landscape a legitimate issue for public debate have failed to do so. Those traditionally qualified to educate the public about our aesthetic condition have been inadequate to the task. Dealing in distinct pieces rather than contextual wholes, they too have become victims of their own overly focused, narrowly parochial perception.

The aesthetic heritage of America is too important to be left in the hands of the usual architectural critics, urban planners, and environmental activists. The New American Landscape will neither be understood nor improved on by the customary tired old observations and clichés about urban design, mass transit, green belt preservation, billboard control, and other shibboleths. Awakening the public to aesthetic issues depends on the ability to understand the true nature of the New American Landscape in all its complexities.

At the very least such a task requires revising old, and establishing new, concepts. We must rethink the tired and restrictive notion that the only truly beautiful landscapes are those of spectacular snowcapped mountains or endless desert vistas, such as may be found in our national parks. Fascinated with the grandeur of Yellowstone and the Grand Canyon, Americans have unduly focused on the spectacle of nature instead of on nature itself. As a result, we have forgotten that natural beauty can be as powerful and compelling in a midwestern woodland as atop alpine peaks.

Nature and natural landscapes are infinitely varied. The Georgia swamp, the native grasses of the Kansas prairie, the watery marshes of Maryland—all possess a natural beauty that, if protected from inappropriate development, can enhance our lives. There are few natural landscapes that do not possess unique and inherent beauty. We should therefore not discount the aesthetic qualities of a natural landscape, such as a cornfield or swamp, because it does not meet some aesthetic test of spectacle and grandeur. Almost all natural landscapes possess aesthetic qualities sorely missing from the man-made environment, and they are by virtue of that reality alone worthy of our recognition.

Once we have broadened our understanding of what constitutes beauty in the natural environment, we can begin the more difficult task of understanding and appreciating what aesthetic qualities yet exist in the man-made environment. It is not necessarily difficult to recognize individual buildings, homes, and other structures that possess pleasing design and aesthetic character. The more difficult and more rewarding task is to identify and understand those rare landscapes, even fragments of landscapes, that combine the natural and the man made. Such unsuspected and delightful juxtapositions impress on us a sum total that far exceeds the separate parts.

Nonetheless, difficult as it is to cite specific examples, locations that combine natural and man-made environments in exceptionally pleasing combinations do come to mind. No one who has traveled to the country villages of Bavaria can fail to be impressed with how unobtrusive and compatible with the countryside they appear. Far from intruding on the natural setting, the typical Bavarian village seems to enhance the natural setting. It adds to the woods and fields a certain benign domesticity and sense of place that a natural landscape, minus the evidence of man's works, would fail to convey. One is reminded that paradise is not paradise without the presence of man.

Dark Satanic Malls

More difficult by far is discovering an American landscape that combines both the natural and the man made in such a way as to create a totality that is aesthetically compelling. Often college and university campuses suggest images of stately, architecturally ornate, academic buildings situated amid trees and bodies of water. The resulting tableau is usually pleasing but often artificial, even contrived. It is as if such a felicitous combination of civilization and nature could only occur in the highly rarefied, if not stylized, confines of a stage-managed environment. Such a description aptly applies to many eastern and midwestern campuses that had their origin as isolated enclaves acting in loco parentis.

It is much more emotionally moving to encounter such a fusion of man and nature within the real time and real space of the urban environment. Let us consider Los Angeles. I mention Los Angeles precisely because it is, more than most American cities, an aesthetically devoid landscape dedicated to utility and the incessant indulgences of innumerable private men. It is in Los Angeles that the potentialities of the New American Landscape seem a future only hours away.

On a recent visit to Los Angeles, I became lost in thickets of billboards and countless fast-food establishments formed in the image of their main entree. Mistakenly, I turned a corner to find myself peering into what seemed like a window on the past. It was a street scene of apartment buildings each in the art deco style of the 1930s. This is not in itself uncommon in Los Angeles. However, individually and collectively these particular buildings on this particular street seemed to belong. They were neither superfluously added nor detracted to over time by thoughtless "improvements." Unlike countless other apartments and offices in Los Angeles, their rooftops contained no billboards. These buildings retained an architectural integrity so artistically powerful as to illicit a swell of nostalgia for a past I had never experienced.

Yet what made the scene so pleasurable, so moving, was a forest of oak trees extending behind, around, and before those handsome apartments. Those trees evoked not merely nostalgia but a fervent connection to a lost natural landscape long ago paved over by the greater city around me. The buildings alone were a memorable architectural experience. The buildings and the trees together created an almost magical space in the midst of a city whose aesthetic excess is strictly black magic.

The existence of magical confluences of man and nature in contexts as unlikely as Los Angeles does not necessarily mean such alluring places will be recognized and preserved. However, it does mean that even a landscape as small as a few buildings on one city block can deeply instill a sense of historic place and a meaningful connection with the natural world.

Alienation, disconnection, and anesthetization may be the most common responses to the utility and commercialization that dominate the American landscape. Yet, the power of place need not be only negative. We do have the capacity to be emotionally attracted to, and enriched by, the physical spaces that surround and define us. We are capable of responding to an environment that is both naturally beautiful and that evokes a historic sense of place and connection to the past.

Despite the evolving domination of the New American Landscape, there exist what can only be considered magical spaces. These territories of the tasteful fuse the best of civilization and nature in a joyful union that calls awake our slumbering aesthetic sense. Yet, questions remain: Will those of us who sleepwalk through dark satanic malls become conscious or remain anesthetized? Are we destined to wander dazed and unknowing amid the elaborate spectacle, munificent enticements, and novel sensations that will be but commonplace on the New American Landscape? We must ask these questions not so much of ourselves as of the New Man who will come to call the New American Landscape home.

25

2 THE NEW MAN
Mimesis and Immanence

The death of the city and of the countryside is an inevitable result of the demise of public man. Public man offered us the example of benign disinterestedness as the most powerful moral alternative to private passions. Public man was the personification of the transcendence of self-interest and self-absorption. As public men, we acknowledged the broader interests of community, of nature, and of God.

Through the ministrations of public man emerged the city's finest hour: the communion of multiple selves in mutual recognition of shared concern. In the countryside, public man understood the dependence and interdependence of the tenuous self on the impersonal forces of nature unfolding with little acknowledgment of human concerns. It was the inherent disinterestedness of public man that made him the age's most likely aesthetician. He understood both the rational and emotive realization of harmony in all of its historical modalities: the harmony of men in communities and of men in nature; and the ultimate notion of aesthetics, the harmony of the soul with God.

Such sublime understanding is dependent on the self-transcendence embodied in the notion of the disinterested public man. But we no longer seriously believe in self-transcendence. In our age of doubt and impatience, public man fails as a concept, not only metaphysically but metaphorically. The tenor of the age is not one that lends itself to claims of the greater good and the general welfare. In the chorus of appeals to our better natures, we are, for lack of a more appropriate word, embarrassed at what strikes us as not so much ideological arrogance but starry-eyed utopian naïveté.

The common sense of Adam Smith's self-interested invisible hand appeals to both our Puritan sense of self-sufficiency and our native skepticism. We are weary of proselytizing do-gooders who have cluttered our history with the cheap baggage of pious moralizing. We are, in our blood, practical people seeking practical solutions. What could be more practical than to consider self-transcendence some untenable romantic mischief, some illusory puff from the dustbin of clichés, a decidedly unscientific notion best dispensed with? After all, modernity itself has subjected each of our transcendent modalities to withering and skeptical review, only to reject them all out of hand.

First to fall from grace was the traditional concept of God. God as a supernatural force capable of appearing in history to act on individual human lives was transformed into abstraction and dogma by the undeniable and irrefutable logic of rationalism. Shortly afterward, the state too was reviled. Its blood lust and political intrigues, its solicitations to patriotism, and its seduction by blatant self-interest demonstrated that appeals to political absolutes could not nurture and sustain the transcendent temperament.

Ironically, in this century the most poignant lesson on the limitations of transcendence is demonstrated in the inherent

27

shortcomings of modernity's bastard children: twentieth-century science and technology. Surely, even the most ardent proponent of technology realizes that emotive and quasi-religious appeals to its inherent righteousness strike us as the moral equivalent of a Hollywood horror film. Better arguments in support of technology would be based on anything other than faith in its ability to bring ultimate meaning to our lives.

Modernity in all its merciless skepticism, cynicism, and realism has invalidated transcendence, stripping it of any claim to legitimacy, shoving its broken and disgraced hulk from further appeals to our consideration. Transcendence of self is finally a concept attractive only to those on the fringe of legitimacy. The marginalizing of self-transcendence refocuses our identity inward. Man no longer imitates God, nor even some generalized Platonic version of man. We have now arrived at that point in history in which man is quite comfortable imitating himself.

As self-transcendence becomes a notion relegated to romantic poets and students of the nineteenth century, the refutation of self-transcendence invalidates relations among the self and others. That which depends on an individual and collective realization of reciprocity—beginning with the notion of community itself—becomes jeopardized.

The disinterestedness of public man clarified and illuminated the pivotal role of reciprocity in maintaining balance on the frontier and in building the city. With the passing of public man, the ethos of reciprocity he instilled is no longer sustainable, and community exists in name and in form but not in substance. With the death of the city and the countryside, real community will fail to endure.

Modernity differs from past epochs. As in other historical periods we can forgo others, reject mutual obligations, and refuse to act as members of communities. We can choose to mock notions of self-transcendence and to imitate not God but man. However, modernity does not provide the choice to forgo others and to embrace the egotism of private sensibilities. Modernity is the negation of that choice and the establishment of no other option. The culminating reality of modernity is that it progressively reduces our options while creating the inevitability of the New American Landscape.

Today a New Man is being born amid the uncertainties and emerging new realities of institutions and organizations in flux. As the New Man emerges on the New American Landscape, the general contours of his consciousness, lifestyle, values, and identity become clear. A major shaper of that identity is psychotherapy. The proliferation of psychotherapy among the American middle class is as much of a dramatic alteration of America's emotional landscape as is the transformation of the physical landscape. The New American Landscape is the outward manifestation of our collective inner selves—best understood as a product of psychotherapeutic values.

Just as Freud thought of himself as a scientist, we tend to think of psychotherapy as a scientific or medically based process to treat those with emotional problems. The objective is to solve the problem and facilitate the person's ability to function with others, to return that person to society. The ostensible point of psychotherapy, especially given its pseudo-scientific and medical character, is to help people function better with those around them. Given that perspective, psychotherapy is seen as a sound method for enriching our lives by educating and sensitizing increasing numbers of people to the potential of productive social interaction.

The practical consequence of the proliferation of psychotherapy reveals a significantly different reality. Previously, psychotherapy seemed to be about the treatment and rehabilitation of individuals with a debilitating pathology. The socially unfit were made socially fit. As increasing numbers of people experience psychotherapy, the percentage that is truly socially dysfunctional is decreasing. Most undergoing psychotherapy today are doing so not because they are unable to interact successfully as social beings but because they desire to act more successfully. The aim of psychotherapy has been transformed from that of rehabilitating people to function in society to "empowering" those who seek to outperform, outcompete, outcreate, and out self-express their fellows. The objective of therapy for most participants is to enhance an individual's social performance, as measured by such criteria as a successful marriage, optimum relations with parents, a lucrative career, and meaningful friendships. In this sense, therapy is less a process dealing with pathology and more a process of self-improvement.

As self-improvement, therapy would serve a useful purpose. However, the social influence and power of therapy are disproportionate to that of self-improvement movements in American history. The decline of traditional sources of normative behavior—such as the church, the school, and the home—create an ethical vacuum. In the wake of their demise, therapy has taken on the job of redefining what we as a society mean when we talk about such fundamental social values as self-interest versus the interests of others. Psychotherapy, steeped in the pretensions of medical and social science, becomes the logical candidate to propagate behavioral values for private men and women interested in maximizing their private objectives. In a society that believes human nature is perfectible, therapy becomes a powerful technological system to enhance our personalities and liberate us from human imperfections.

The ability of therapy to reorder and restructure society is clear. In the past, the home, the church, and the school defined the individual in terms of the larger society. Today, therapy defines the larger society in terms of the individual. It is no surprise that therapy has substituted the "I" of the individual for the "we" of the broader community. Therapy has placed the individual, not the social community, at the center of the therapeutic universe. All else follows from this fundamental reality. In this basic way psychotherapy has legitimized our society's propensity for narcissistic self-indulgence.

Therapy is the application of behavioral technology toward the objective of creating a New Man who will become the dominant resident of the New American Landscape. Such new men, when necessary, will undergo psychotherapy for treatment of socially dysfunctional pathologies. Much more often they will consume therapy, like any other commodity, to enhance social performance. Therapy will heal and rehabilitate the socially sick. Moreover, given enough time, money, and expertise, therapy will have the potential to improve the social performance of an entire society of individuals. They will be encouraged and motivated by therapy to act increasingly as individuals first and as members of social

31

communities a distant second. Therapy is the seminal mechanism for the transformation of public into private values and for the creation of the New Man.

How did we transform from a society that attempted to balance group and individual rights and responsibilities to a society that seems consumed with individual excess? In the past, the individual was defined in relation to the greater social whole. We progressed historically from the notion of family to that of tribe, then community, then nation. Each step of the way, an individual alone, without social connection and social definition, was literally unthinkable to the eighteenth- and nineteenth-century theorists of individual liberty. Liberty for individuals was possible only within a societal context. The individual alone was not free but licentious.

However, today we are returning to an age of individuals unfettered by, and without benefit of, mediating social context. Over the past fifty years the concept of the individual, defined as part of the social whole, has devolved, some might say mutated, into the concept of the megaself. This powerful megaself perverts the notion of individualism by negating moral, religious, and ethical restraints on individual behavior. Instead, the megaself postulates a worldview in which self-autonomy is the preferred means to achieving private ends.

The publication of Robert N. Bellah's *Habits of the Heart: Individualism and Commitment in American Life* in the mid-1980s renewed attention on the dramatically lessening influence of communal and group values on individual behavior. Once church, school, neighborhood, family, and the workplace all provided a mechanism to guide, comfort, nurture, and discipline the individual. It is in the twentieth century, blessed by psychology and psychotherapy, full production and full consumption, universal education, and mass media, that the emergence of the autonomous self has come to define the American post-industrial consumer society.

Today's consumer-driven, comfort-obsessed, rights-promulgating, self-gratifying way of life is hardly life within a society. Rather, it is the life of a loose confederation of autonomous and anonymous individuals interacting in the marketplace of commodities, lovers, and therapies. These individuals rely on government to referee and keep the playing field level and to facilitate expeditious competition among rival self-interests. In such a society, increasing degrees of fiscal, physical, and psychic energy are expended in identifying, examining, caring for, and catering to the self. The prescription—help yourself—is both an incantation and an evocation of the zeitgeist of the age.

Energies once invested in the general welfare, as it has been historically and traditionally defined, are now increasingly reserved for those mechanisms and institutions that acknowledge the supreme importance of the self. Television is the world's dominant form of communication and great destroyer of literacy. There can be no better example of creating and catering to the autonomous megaself while effecting the illusion, but not the reality, of what pundit Marshall McLuhan called the global village.

We are able to communicate instantly and with little regard for the barriers of time and space. However, we have substituted the immediacy and pervasiveness of communications technology for the intimacy and meaning of genuine human interaction. Conventional wisdom suggests that the average

33

The New Man

American watches over six hours of television daily. No one can argue that whatever the number of hours, such time necessarily isolates and insulates the viewer from the real world. Tragically, increasing numbers of global village residents are becoming village idiots, their pathology measured not just by their illiteracy but by their autonomy and atomism.

We justify social change in terms of the unfulfilled, denied, and legitimate needs and aspirations of the primordial life force we call the self. This megaself, not the broader community, society, or nation, has become the dominant measure of ultimate concern and ultimate value.

Of course, our history has been shaped and defined by a continuous acknowledgment of obligations and responsibilities to the greater good. Merely a generation ago, the clichéd answer to the meaning of existence was to provide the next generation with the means to a better life. Today, such a remark is not merely a cliché. It reminds us of a society that no longer exists. In such a society there were those for whom the pursuit of beauty, the desire for knowledge, the need to understand ideas were in themselves reasons to be. Most alien to our present sensibilities, there was a time when human existence was seen by many as a sacred obligation to understand the demands and expectations of God, an opportunity to acquire grace.

Where once the pursuit of pleasure was honestly acknowledged for the hedonism it was, today the pursuit of self-gratification is deemed a sign of mental and emotional health. Therapists advise us to get in touch with our feelings, not with our sense of ethics. Educators lecture us that students need to develop self-esteem, not their intellectual capabilities. Spiritual healers, on public television no less, caution us to attend to the needs of our inner child, rather than minister to the needs of inner-city children.

Above all else we are encouraged to express ourselves rather than think twice before we subject others to our ill-considered and uninformed opinions. We have in our lifetimes lived through a cultural substitution of self-excess for self-restraint. Once humility required modesty. Today, those ill-suited to self-promotion—whether in business, social, or romantic endeavors—are considered, not virtuous in curbing their immodesty, but the victim of their own timidity.

But even self-promotion has given way to self-confession as the ultimate act of self-expression. Why must we bear witness to one more bumper sticker proclaiming that some insecure person loves his or her dog? Such bumper sticker exclamations are an example of an unwarranted presumption of interest where none exists. The desire to reveal oneself on one's bumper sticker demonstrates the self's pathological obsession with confession, when confession is neither elicited nor even acknowledged. Ours is a society in which many know of Freudian psychology but few of Freud's contention that civilization is a function of suppression, not indulgence, of our pathetic little personalities yearning for self-expression.

Today, in the popular imagination, in the world as defined by mass media, life is simply and undeniably the pursuit of self-gratification. Even contemporary criticisms of materialism, such as we encounter on television talk shows, are based on the supposition that the time it takes to acquire wealth is time taken away from real self-enjoyment. What is most peculiar about this affirmation of the importance of having fun above all else is how unpeculiar it seems, how comfortable it fits. For the popular mind is incapable of imagining a more compelling reason to get up every morning than the pursuit of what feels good.

The emergence of the New American Landscape is a function of the New Man who embodies the undeniable and irrefutable megaself. This point of view suggests that our environment is pathologically out of balance because we are out of balance. Much to the chagrin of the advocates of personal growth, we are particularly unbalanced in our pursuit of what we now consider virtue, as well as in our seduction by vice. Such is another version of the classic old adage: the road to hell is paved with good intentions.

The death of the city, the countryside, and the aesthetic sensibility poses a significant moral question for the New Man. Of what is he a part? From whom and what is his meaning derived? In what sense, if any, is he defined by others? Put another way, what has meaning on the New American Landscape?

Meaning for the New Man is defined within, not outside, the megaself. Meaning is not transcendent of human experience but immanent within human experience. The New Man is therefore entirely self-created and self-referential. Reciprocity has been eclipsed, not merely by self-interest but by self-invention and perpetual reinvention. Modernity gives rise to the birth of the New Man and the New American Landscape.

To whom do we turn in seeking help to further illuminate the nature of the New Man and his symbiotic relationship to the New American Landscape? Certainly not psychotherapists, for they have abdicated questions of ultimate ethical and moral concern in favor of perfecting technique. Certainly not educators, who are preoccupied with the final stages of the admittedly painful and traumatic transformation of our educational system. It is a transformation from teaching the values of public man to facilitating the private fulfillment of our individual desires. Schools, at all levels, exist to help us get better jobs, to earn greater incomes, to consume more products and services. Once, our educational institutions clearly demonstrated we were a distinct American culture defined by the concerns of public man. Today, education clearly demonstrates that we are less members of a culture than members of an economy.

And we would certainly not turn to the established church. Members of the clergy seem more concerned with accommodating popular passions of the day than acknowledging that the moral world as we know it has come to an end. No, to understand the true significance of the New Man and the New American Landscape we must turn to explorers of the metaphorical environment.

3 THE NEW AMERICAN LANDSCAPE
Ego and Egotopia

inguists like to say that it is our ability to speak metaphorically, to compare dissimilar things by alleging an
unsuspected similarity, that is the defining characteristic
of human intellectual proclivity. Some might contend that
metaphorical interpretation is a function of what we have
come to consider the classical literary imagination and, therefore, in this age of cyberspace, is a capability in irreversible
decline. Others would not hesitate to suggest that a pervasive
literalism, most certainly an unintended but debilitating by-
product of our television culture, has diminished our ability
to metaphorically interpret what is happening in the physical
environment.

The New American Landscape defies the traditional analysis of architects, planners, and environmentalists. Their narrowly focused, piecemeal view impedes a comprehensive
contextual understanding of the great suburban transformation. Pathetically, they continue to see only discrete components—a historic building in need of preservation here, a
neighborhood in need of renewal there, a wetland or potential open space that needs to be saved. Whatever, and however noble, the objective, the process is essentially a reaction

to forces essentially beyond the understanding of those who concern themselves with land-use planning, environmental regulations, building codes, and other such esoterica.

The New American Landscape can only be understood by those possessing a metaphoric sensibility. The pernicious invisibility of a synthetic environment, whose purpose is to facilitate and encourage consumption and possibly other activities by its unaware and unknowing inhabitants, is a subject perhaps best comprehended by artists, writers, and those capable of imagination. For it is only the power of imagination in the service of intellect that is capable of comprehending such an American landscape that, even a few short years ago, would have been considered unimaginable.

To elucidate the meaning of our emerging national landscape, one is indebted to the late Marshall McLuhan, whose popularized identity as a media guru belied his credentials as a master of literary analysis. McLuhan's lifelong interest in the metaphoric insights of James Joyce, especially in the seminal novel *Finnegans Wake,* served as a basis for McLuhan's own now-famous dictum, "the medium is the message." McLuhan should be remembered, but not for what many think he had to say about the nature of television. How he defined public consciousness is important. McLuhan playfully used television to illustrate that the public's collective consciousness during any particular era is a function of the dominant form of communication.

For McLuhan, in the age of print the public's collective consciousness became a product of the characteristics of print technology—that is, linear, selective and visually discriminating, individual and temporal. In McLuhan's view the individualism of the print-dominated nineteenth century was no accident and very much analogous to the selective and discrete functionality of the human eye that print technology imitated. With the coming of electronic media in the twentieth century, McLuhan contended that our collective consciousness no longer is a product of the characteristics of print technology but of television—that is, nonlinear, immediate, visually indiscriminate, collective, and transtemporal. The analogy this time was not to the human eye but to the human nervous system.

Given the change in dominant media, McLuhan contended that the twentieth century would witness the decline of blatant individualism and a reemergence of collective and communal values. McLuhan's conclusions can be disputed, given the continuing ascendancy of individual over group values. The point is to understand that he interpreted both communications technology and public consciousness metaphorically. His was not the one-dimensional analysis of insecure social scientists. He was not attempting to emulate what is perceived to be the superior and quantifiable method of the physical sciences in understanding social and cultural phenomena.

What can only be considered McLuhan's devilish playfulness in presenting his elaborate theories confounded both his critics and admirers, most of whom had no idea what he was talking about. They still do not. It is McLuhan, more than many in recent memory, whose essentially metaphoric probing of current realities disturbed complacent fellow academicians. He gave us the means of awakening the public from its collective unconsciousness by understanding how communications technology influences public thinking and behavior. McLuhan's legacy encouraged others to attempt to define the nature of the media and to probe its impact. My intention is to offer McLuhan's metaphorical method as a model to understand and evaluate not just the media but the very real impact of the New American Landscape on our lifestyle, values, and identity.

As surely as an archaeologist painstakingly unearths layers of history, our physical environment reveals to the metaphoric sensibility a transformation. We have been transformed from a society modeled on the professed virtues of balance, harmony, rights, and responsibilities to one that unabashedly celebrates excessive behavior and self-indulgence in the name of self-liberation. Put another way, the ugliness of our environment is a function of our transformation from a society of communal values to one that celebrates and encourages individual self-indulgence. Greed, ignorance, mindless science and technology, and excessive materialism contribute to both environmental destruction and a public confusion and ambiguity about aesthetics. Far more disturbing is the view that our allegedly enlightened values, notably self-worth, self-actualization, and the ever popular self-expression, create the occasion for environmental and aesthetic degeneration.

41

The New American Landscape is a metaphor for, and physical evidence of, the decline of community values and the ascension of the megaself. Volumes have been written chronicling the sprawling, brawling, ungainly suburb, the favorite target for critics identifying our social and political excesses. In a historically brief fifty years, America has turned its back on community, as community has been traditionally defined, and embraced the suburban cultural breeding ground of self-absorption.

The New American Landscape

Just as cathedrals were a symbol of what was valued most in medieval society, the New American Landscape embodies what today's society values most: the consumption of goods and services as the means for defining self-identity. Some may call the New American Landscape a community, but it is much more a community of consumption than of reciprocal obligations and responsibilities among its members. The ubiquitous opportunity to consume is at the heart of the New American Landscape, which is a declaration of the ultimate importance of the megaself. The New American Landscape is the physical transformation of public space into a literal marketplace for which surely there is no economic necessity and every evidence of psychological obsession.

In years past, the marketplace was clearly defined and physically limited. The physical space and influence of the family, the neighborhood, the school, and the church stood distinctly uncompromised by the attractions and seductions of the market. In the New American Landscape, designed to enhance self-indulgence, the entire society must become literally a perpetual, omnipresent, round-the-clock market. The consuming self must be free to pursue self-creation, self-renewal, and self-redemption through the unfettered act of spontaneous consumption.

To the metaphoric sensibility consumption is our process of defining self-identity. Identity-building through consumption satisfactorily explains such physical phenomena as the proliferation of outdoor advertising; the social acceptance of advertising messages on clothing; and even, through indoor billboards, the commercialization of public rest rooms. Critics of advertising and rampant consumerism miss the point when they suggest that such persuasions convince the ma-

The New American Landscape

nipulated masses to buy what they neither need nor want. What we are dealing with is not so much the evidence of a Madison Avenue conspiracy haranguing us to buy snake oil as our collective cultural need to be the constant recipients of instructions in the liturgy of consumption.

For a people whose identity increasingly depends on what they consume, advertising messages are no longer irritating, intrusive, and inane but informative, sustaining, and nurturing. It is no more likely for the New Man to object to the ubiquitous presence of advertising in his environment than it would have been for a medieval parishioner to object to the presence of Christian symbols in his village. We are not free from ubiquitous advertising messages because we do not want to be free. How could we function in a physical environment in which the ability to consume was not an omnipresent opportunity for self-expression and the formation and renewal of self-identity?

So what is the metaphor to be understood within the enigma of our environment? Mircea Eliade asserted in *The Sacred and the Profane: The Nature of Religion* that the sacred environment of the prehistoric tribe was compromised by the profanity of an emerging modernity. The physical world was de-sanctified. God was abstracted and banished to a non-physical realm (Heaven) so that the environment would be available for the erection of shopping malls that could not have been constructed were such real estate occupied by sacred deities. Eliade's line of reasoning is taken several precarious steps further toward an unfathomable abyss, as today's physical environment has become not merely profane but obscene, in the twisted plasticity of self-gratification.

Case in point. When today one reads the southern agrarians—Allen Tate, Robert Penn Warren, John Crowe Ransom, Stark Young—that band of prophets whose *I'll Take My Stand* first appeared in 1930 as a defense of southern agriculture against the onslaught of northern industrialism, one is confronted repeatedly with the notion that southerners, above all others, have a loving, almost spiritual relationship with the land. This love for the land is an inherent appreciation for the potentialities and the limitations of the organic, in both husbandry and the business of the state. It transfixes the southern agrarian sensibility so dramatically, so comprehensively, on the notion of limits on both the self and the society at large.

The agrarians stood helplessly in the face of industrialism and evoked their love for the land, an act that made them eerie precursors of contemporary environmentalists. The irony, of course, is that today the American South, the homeland of those who profess a special, unique, and peculiarly southern love and respect for the land, is unquestionably the most aesthetically debased environment in the United States, with the possible exceptions of Los Angeles and Las Vegas. There can be no more compelling argument that our beloved landscape reflects our self-image writ large than a drive from the Midwest to Disney World, southward down Interstate 75, where endless roadside blight evokes the admiration of tourist and resident alike.

To the metaphoric sensibility, the self has become the environment. Put another way, the self has appropriated the environment for the undeniable purpose of self-idolatry. This is hardly surprising in what Christopher Lasch calls the culture of narcissism. While some propose that the Earth is, in fact, a living organism, the inescapable conclusion of the meta-

The New American Landscape

phoric sensibility affirms that, if the Earth is anything, it has assumed the burden of the self. It has become our individual, primordial, id-driven self. Much like Christ was crucified for our sins, the Earth itself has now become the crucified Christ.

We have arrived at this moment in history, having exhausted our political resources as we have our psychic energy. Inadvertently, and from different motivations, liberals and conservatives have transformed the traditional and historic community of responsible individuals by substituting a confederation of autonomous selves unnurtured by social obligations to the greater good. The man of the hour stands among us: disassociated, disenfranchised, disaffected, disillusioned, disinclined, and diseased.

What other outcome was possible given the death of God, the destruction of the ancient regime, the handy dismissal of bourgeois middle-class morality, the final and complete negation of authority of almost every type? While so-called conservatives reject so-called liberal values, they have substituted the morality and authority of the market for traditional virtues. If nothing else, history has taught apparently everyone but the political conservatives the revolutionary power of the market to destroy tradition, to displace long-held values, and to free individuals from age-old restraints on behavior.

The materialism of the market, more than liberal flirtation with free thinking and free love, has destroyed "family values" (so important to some conservatives). The materialism of the market has transformed the spiritual and the transcendent from a source of civic virtue to merely another commodity to be purchased at weekend meditation workshops and from purveyors of self-help manuals. If humility, piety,

The New American Landscape

stability, polity, and civility depend on restraining the passions of the id, then the market is a poor mechanism for keeping the lid on the id. It is hardly credible for political conservatives, embracing market values, to blame political liberals for the relativism and amorality of modernity.

While modern conservatives have expanded the notion of the market by substituting market values for all other values, contemporary liberals have contributed to the destruction of the concept of individual responsibility by denying the validity of individual volition and exaggerating the influence of institutions. The liberal's answer to the demise of communal values and the proliferation of atomistic and autonomous individuals is to portray them as victims of some institutional, cultural, social, or economic conspiracy. All such theories rob individuals of their need to take responsibility for their actions and their identity.

"We are all Keynesians now," Richard Nixon once commented about the influence of liberal British economist John Maynard Keynes, even on conservative economists. Similarly, the metaphorical interpretation of today's political reality suggests that, whatever our present circumstances, they are a function of bipartisan abdication of the stuff that gave meaning to such currently meaningless values as character, integrity, duty, service, and obligation. Above all else, we have abandoned the restraint of excessive personal behavior. Such abandonment is the single most defining characteristic of our age of self-absorption.

Columnist George Will once alluded that the government should do more than grease the skids of commerce while leaving ethics to the philosophers. In reality it is not just government but the cultural infrastructure as well that, in the em-

The New American Landscape

brace of market-driven values, has abandoned ethics to the philosophers. To the metaphoric sensibility, the market is, of course, a metaphor for the triumph of the self over the many. The triumph of the megaself and the elevation of private above public interests was not exactly what socially concerned and morally obligated Adam Smith had in mind when he spoke of the virtues of free enterprise in *The Wealth of Nations.*

Unfortunately for the literal-minded, we as a society are increasingly incapable of seeing and understanding the hidden metaphorical environment. We have not only increasingly lost our ability to see and understand metaphorically, we have lost our sense of history, have forgotten much of our sense of continuity that links the precarious and sinister present with the defined and defining past.

The New American Landscape is radically different from past environments. Its driving and defining reality—the need to increase aggregate consumption of goods and services, facilitated by a therapeutic emphasis on the individual at the expense of the community—has pushed from public discourse and consciousness any competing interests, no matter how historically compelling. The great issues of the day are defined and interpreted to fit within this paradigm.

In an age of narcissism in which data are confused with information and information mistaken for knowledge, history is indeed dead. Literature depends on literacy, which, if one is generous, can be said to have evolved into an appreciation for film and video. Art has been distorted, appropriated, and put in the service of financial gain. Politics is ridiculed and demeaned. Religion has been co-opted by psychotherapy and the growing industry of self-improvement. Science and technology continue to be simultaneously lusted after for their ability to contribute economically and to perfect our protean personalities and feared because of their destructive capabilities.

Who can convincingly argue against the notion that ours has become a society in which the economy and economic matters alone subsume all other values? Ironically, economics is even the master of therapy, whose primary function no longer is to treat the sick but to enhance individual social and business performance. In that fundamental way, therapy serves as an agent of economic values deep in the heart of our personal, private, and ostensibly noneconomic concerns.

In a society in which economic matters are indisputably supreme, land management, construction, and advertising technologies have become increasingly sophisticated. As noted, our mastery of psychological and sociological systems must be considered equally sophisticated insofar as these technologies manage and manipulate people. It should come as no surprise that a New American Landscape, unnatural, ahistorical, and synthetic in character, should arise to facilitate, orchestrate, and encourage aggregate consumption of goods and services.

In the nineteenth and early twentieth centuries the environment was affected most greatly by the presence of the industrial forces of production. Today, the forces of consumption—more subtle, more diffuse, and decentralized; and in so being, much more powerful in their ability to influence—dominate the emerging landscape of the great suburban transformation.

If consumption drives the consumer economy, information, particularly advertising, drives consumption and has the capacity to accelerate the pace of consumption. This is the classic criticism of advertising, and it has only become more—not less—convincing over the years. It should come as no surprise to students of marketing, advertising, and promotion that innovative marketers are always searching for new and supplemental channels of communication to cost-effectively reach decision makers and consumers in the market (or should be if they are earning their pay). Once the obvious media—television, radio, billboards, films, magazines—are successfully and effectively utilized, and once older, dying media—such as newspapers—are strategically abandoned, new media such as the Internet are developed or appropriated to reach audiences. Using the Internet to disseminate sales information and advertising is just one example of technology spawning new advertising channels.

49

The ability for advertisers in a very real sense to appropriate and use the physical environment to encourage, orchestrate, and stimulate increased levels of consumption is a concept that is not the stuff of science fiction but a proposition to be taken seriously. Theoretically, if not practically, the ideal physical environment of the market for a marketer of consumer goods would be as plastic, as fluid, as changeable, as immediate, and as susceptible to incorporating advertising messages, both unobtrusively and overtly, as is television itself.

The New American Landscape is such an environment, and it has become one of history's most persuasive and successful advertising media, second only to television. Our environment has become a larger-than-life television commercial projected to us and through us by billboards, shopping malls, the design of our streets and thoroughfares, and on the ubiquitous American highway that is the destination common to all of America.

Our environment, both at home and away, has become a medium through which subtle and not so subtle advertising messages encourage us to consume. We, as motorists, as pedestrians at the shopping mall, as students in school forced to watch TV commercials in the classroom, are the audience. As residents of neighborhoods with billboards and advertising posters on bus stops and telephone booths we are the collective and individual audience forever to be enticed and seduced by a theatrical and commercial environment to a life of infinite consumption. For all practical purposes, and certainly from an aesthetic viewpoint, the environment has become the Yellow Pages.

We are well aware of the now classic argument that advertising forces people to buy what they neither need nor even want. Rest assured that it is not my intention to suggest that America's advertisers have consciously conspired to so construct and design the American landscape with the deliberate intent to manipulate the American public into buying what it otherwise would not. Such arguments, whether they apply to television commercials or to the physical landscape itself, are simplistic and one-dimensional and hardly provide us with the insight we need to understand how people are influenced and what to do about it.

What makes the influence and persuasive ability of the New American Landscape so powerful and so troubling is that its impact is not the conscious and deliberate work of Madison Avenue conspirators. Big business has neither the capability nor the imagination to even begin successfully designing and constructing an environment with the power to subconsciously influence people's habits and patterns of consumption. There is no individual entity—business, academic, or governmental—with the capability of doing so.

The power and persuasive ability of the New American Landscape to influence our consumptive behavior, and possibly other behavior as well, is the result of the fifty-year evolution of the great suburban transformation. Collectively and individually, we as a society must all share responsibility for the character of the nation's rapidly emerging environment. Of course, having said that, one must also point out that certain groups, such as the billboard industry, must share a greater responsibility for the more overt excesses corrupting the environment. However, it is a mistake to believe the New American Landscape to be anything less than the physical manifestation of the consciousness of the New Man who is the primary resident of that landscape.

As we have seen, the New American Landscape is neither natural, historical, nor accidental. It is ultimately a synthetic creation, as is the New Man himself. The New Man is a fabrication infused with, and unquestioningly accepting, a literal need to achieve the perfectibility of his protean personality. In so doing he seeks to fulfill his private and individual desires. The New Man and the New American Landscape are in a state of perpetual mutability and constant motion, pledged to accommodate the will to perfection.

To best understand the environment of Egotopia, we must force ourselves to endure the single most disturbing prospect one who appreciates aesthetic beauty can contemplate—to actually encounter our fellows in travels about our land. On the great American highway, through the New American Landscape, the journey, in all its depravity, is the reward. To

The New American Landscape

the metaphoric sensibility, the American highway reveals, in unforgiving detail, the psyche of the New Man. The American highway is our self-defining moment. Out there on the highway, what you see reshaping the environment is the physical manifestation of who we have become.

52

4 THE MYTH OF TRAVEL AND THE NECESSITY OF MOTION

Those of us born in the 1940s grew up in a decade, the 1950s, curiously influenced by an event that occurred before our birth: the Great Depression. No single experience, perhaps not even the Second World War, made such a lasting impact on my parents and their friends. Though my generation was to be called, among other things, the first generation of affluence, my parents could never really believe the depression was over. They were fearful of economic deprivation, no matter how much their income grew in the booming postwar economy. To them the depression lurked menacingly like a crazy relative locked in the attic, plotting a threatening and potentially dangerous reappearance.

Buying that house in the suburbs, getting that new car, trying out installment buying, spending money like it had not been spent since the 1920s—my parents and their generation, which were to be the pioneers of the great suburban transformation, did not hesitate to spend their way to happiness. In the dramatic postwar birth of American suburbia, those who personally experienced the depression needed to believe they were buying more than goods and services. They were building a new era of never-ending prosperity.

The expenditures that paid for 1950s postwar opulence and suburban expansion were seen by the suburban pioneers as the nation investing in a lifestyle that would be somehow depression-proof. The more they secretly feared the return of the depression, the more each new household purchase, each new suburban development, school, and shopping center, was to be physical evidence of an indisputable and immutable affluence. In a sense, the suburban transformation was to be proof of the nation's serious commitment to the promise of prosperity first comprehensively spelled out in the Full Employment Act of 1946. There was to be no turning back to a time when just plain folks would be victims of economic cycles over which they had no control.

Like the giant dams then transforming the West's free-flowing rivers into stagnant lakes and environmentally denigrated water channels, the physical reality of the proliferating American suburb in the 1950s was a testament to the nation's love affair with bigness. There was no more effective way to stave off the return of depression than thinking big. Americans wanted to live in big houses and drive big cars. Suburban communities vied with one another for who could tout the biggest regional shopping center. Barry Goldwater was then a popular and colorful U.S. senator. From the air he would look down on some chemical refinery, strip mine, or steel mill and ask his airborne companions, "Is it big enough to get the job done?"

As the 1950s turned into the 1960s, my parents' generation appropriated and celebrated what it perceived to be the successive accomplishments of the great suburban transformation: central air conditioning; the second family car; the out-of-state vacation; and, of course, color television. All were seen as further and continued proof that the American way of life had triumphed over the prospect of economic crisis. Their deep-seated fear of economic depression drove the suburban pioneers to seek perpetual reassurance that the suburban world they had earnestly and enthusiastically created would stand the test of time. Such need motivated the ostentation and obsession with status symbols that so characterized the suburbs of my youth. For the early suburban pioneers, one was not born into suburbia. One's place in the great suburban transformation was purchased. Identity was a function of purchase. The more one purchased and made that purchase obvious to others, the greater one's sense of identity.

55

The suburban pioneers created the physical and economic foundations of the great suburban transformation. Big tract houses, big malls, and big television screens are what they understood best. Their successors have taken much of the suburban infrastructure for granted while adding considerable hardware of their own: cellular phones in their cars, fax machines at home, a computer on-line. Most significantly, the first-generation pioneers of the great suburban transformation have bequeathed authorship of the suburban mythology to those born and brought up on the New American Landscape. As successive generations know only the suburban experience, the mythology of suburbia evolves to reflect their deepening sense of disconnectedness and narcissism. They accept therapeutic values as a means of compensation.

Today's suburban American fears economic recession but is just as fearful of psychological depression. His suburban world is made meaningful to him as a contemporary version of the big thinking of the past. The symbolic value of the sweeping tail fin of 1950s vintage cars has been replaced by

The Myth of Travel

the much more compelling mythic value of the weekly therapy session. Certainly among the most dominant of our contemporary suburban myths is that of the healing power of travel. Travel is the preferred means to soothe the stressed-out psyche while at the same time presenting the opportunity for truly creative and self-renewing opportunities to consume. For the New Man there is no more accepted and encouraged self-indulgence than to recreate by traveling across the New American Landscape.

If one can choose to examine only a single manifestation of how we travel, it must be how we Americans consume our national parks. When asked to name the government agency believed to be doing the best job, we name the National Park Service and give it high marks. The Park Service, because of its effort to preserve and protect our national parks, is everybody's favorite government entity—everybody, that is, but knowledgeable critics who believe that the parks are being loved to death by too many tourists, who in turn are encouraged by a park service more concerned with visitor accommodations than resource protection.

In 1990 there were 258 million visits to areas administered by the National Park Service. What does this remarkable affection for America's parks really mean? Is this impressive and growing number of park visitors an indication that a sizable number of Americans are dedicated conservationists with an evolving and increasingly sophisticated appreciation for the natural environment? Certainly conventional wisdom would have us believe that increased park visitation is the first step in the process of turning park visitors into park defenders and eventually hard-core environmentalists. So the theory goes.

The Myth of Travel

To the metaphorical sensibility, the real meaning of park visitation is nebulous at best. History tells us that the first national parks, Yosemite in California and Yellowstone in Wyoming, were not created to protect valuable ecosystems, save threatened wildlife, or enhance biodiversity. The motivation to set aside America's early national parks was to preserve the scenery from immediate desecration by uncontrolled tourism and other commercial activities. In its earliest days, the American conservation movement was largely a movement to preserve and protect what conservation jargon calls scenic values.

To today's hard-core environmentalist, the desire to protect scenery seems quaint and innocent when compared to compelling ecological reasons to preserve natural resources. Though contemporary park visitors may be motivated as much by scenery as their nineteenth-century predecessors, it is incorrect to attribute today's record park visitations to a developing public appreciation for aesthetics or the environment.

Partly because primitive conditions forced them to and partly because they wanted to experience nature on its own terms, early visitors to our national parks actually interacted with the natural environment. They did not view scenery so much as they were physically and emotionally immersed in it. The majority of today's visitors to America's national parks interact with the natural environment on their terms, not those of nature. They drive when they might walk. They spend more time dining and drinking and shopping at park concessions than they spend hiking on park trails. Such visitor preoccupation with the commercial assets of national parks is well documented. I am reminded of a story about a

The Myth of Travel

tourist at Lake Tahoe who wandered into a local casino and asked a man at the slot machine how to get to the lake. "What lake?" the man responded.

Ironically, the emphasis on accommodating visitors in the style to which they are accustomed has not meant the proliferation of luxury accommodations throughout the national park system. True to form, the facilities at America's national parks are being designed to appeal to the great American middle class that chooses to lodge at economy motels and dine at fast-food chains rather than experience truly elegant accommodations. At a time when the parks are being managed to accommodate visitors at the expense of resource protection, is it not ironic that truly excellent food and fine accommodations are often not available?

As an aging backpacker who has hiked in many of our national parks, I would sometimes welcome the opportunity to leave my tent at home and sleep beneath a roof under the stars. With very few exceptions, such as the Ahwahnee Hotel in Yosemite National Park, food and lodging operations in the parks are designed exclusively to serve the indiscriminate tourist. Mediocre cuisine, mediocre lodging, and mediocre service are the norm. The discriminating, upscale nature lover must endure the frustration of experiencing first-class natural beauty and no-class accommodations all in the same day.

Much more to the point is the presence of both the public's desire to "view" scenery in a national park and the equally strong intention to do so comfortably and conveniently, without having to invest too much time or perspiration. Such curious nature appreciation is practiced by an old friend of mine. His idea of a splendid family vacation is to fly from the East Coast to the West, rent a car, and drive hundreds of miles each day to experience some scenic vista. Upon arriving, my friend and his family jump from the car, furiously take photographs, wolf down something at the nearest fast-food concession, then pile in the car to drive another 300 miles to the next notable scenic vista, where they repeat the orgy of photo taking and imbibing. And so it goes for each of the six to ten days of my friend's annual vacation in America's national parks. I am afraid that for the majority of Americans visiting our parks, my friend's experience of the environment is well understood, even familiar.

By emphasizing visitor convenience, expediency, and comfort, we have made the national park synonymous with the theme park. In the national park the theme is scenery, not experiencing the environment on its own terms. Park visitors consume scenery in our national parks much as they consume the obviously synthetic scenery in a Disney World jungle. The experience is easy and painless, no matter the visitor's age, physical condition, or mental preparation for his visit. Under such circumstances, park visitors are not meaningfully *in* the natural environment so much as *watching* the environment, as if it were on television instead of before their eyes.

What makes the typical park visitor's behavior so ordinary is that it is no different than if he or she were visiting the neighborhood mall or spending an afternoon at home before the television. The typical park visitor makes no special preparations for his or her visit and reads and studies no literature about the park. The typical visitor expects his or her experience to be no different (except not as satisfying) than watching on television a nature program, in which the animals are guaranteed to appear. Such expectations are what distinguish today's park visitors from their historic predecessors.

In no way does this kind of park visitation turn tourists into environmentalists or encourage their understanding of, or appreciation for, aesthetics. Park visitation is a process that appeals to and supports the concept of nature as spectacle. The biggest redwood tree ("I wonder how many picnic tables that sucker would make?"). The highest waterfall. The deepest canyon. The tallest mountain. The hottest desert. And so on. This is nature as spectacle, nature as superlative, and it is what today's increased park visitation is really all about. For the serious television viewer, what other way could nature possibly be experienced and appreciated but to be painlessly, easily, quickly, and visually consumed?

It was as an undergraduate that I began to harbor a peculiar and, to me, ominously disturbing apprehension regarding travel. Though I cannot recall to what extent I would have been able to articulate my concern, indisputably, even in my early 20s, I was at best ambivalent about traveling. One must realize that the young tend to be particularly enamored of travel. Apparently they always have been. Undoubtedly, they tell their parents, and even themselves, that the desire to travel is for the most noble of purposes: observing new and different cultures, negating the threat of provincialism, and, perhaps most important in today's vernacular, creating the occasion for personal growth. I am certain that for many of the young, travel today continues to be what it was during my undergraduate days: an opportunity to take someone far

The Myth of Travel

enough out of town that there is absolutely no chance upon nightfall of not having to share a motel room together.

Being not only young and glandular, I was also sensitive to what I thought travel was really all about. Even in my early 20s, perhaps particularly in my early 20s, travel was supposed to be the opportunity to see and experience that which one could not see and experience at home. Like others of my generation I shared a real passion for the theatrical feature films of the 1930s and 1940s. In such films, travel was a major reoccurring theme in which the protagonist often discovered him- or herself by discovering America.

Who could forget, from Preston Sturges's 1941 classic *Sullivans Travels,* Joel McCray's slander of the residents of the city of Pittsburgh? With absolute certainty he contended that they deserved condemnation because Pittsburgh, in its steel mill ugliness, was so terrible, so unspeakable, so intolerable as to richly deserve rebuke. Nor can the old movie fan not remember with fondness Barbara Stanwick and Fred MacMurry traveling by car from New York City to a farm in southern Indiana in *Remember the Night.* Losing their way on the highway, they were forced to deal with the lovable yet distinctly provincial denizens of a small, genuinely isolated, midwestern hamlet. Certainly Michael J. Fox in *Doc Hollywood* was unable to so convince us of the credibility of his abduction by small-town America.

As a young man in my 20s, travel was supposed to be a liberating experience. It was the opportunity for an undergraduate to embrace existential realities both physical and abstract. Yet to travel through a landscape that was essentially the same as one's neighborhood was not to travel at all. To travel through a landscape that was an unchanging constant of motels, service stations, fast-food outlets, and billboards was not to experience the unique and the different. It was to become bored and irritated with the bleakly familiar.

With a sense of incredulity and undeniable aggravation my friends and I arrived for spring break in Fort Lauderdale. Exhausted after a frenetic trip by car to that collegiate mecca, and anxious for a glimpse of the exotic, we instead were witness to a large illuminated billboard advising that we FLY TO NEW YORK CITY. I had paid good money and spent precious time believing that Fort Lauderdale was a destination worthy of the effort. To be greeted before all else by an invitation to travel to the decidedly unbeachlike, untropical, unnatural city of New York was a psychic intrusion on my exotic Floridian fantasy of the first magnitude. I could not imagine a trench-coated Humphrey Bogart stepping from Rick's Bar in Casablanca to encounter a large illuminated billboard advising that he FLY TO NEW YORK CITY. For me, ever after, no matter to what extent I might have enjoyed that holiday in the sun, Fort Lauderdale was not to be remembered as a distinct and unique location. In my mind it was to be just another place on the great American highway to somewhere else.

How innocent, how naive, yet how prescient do those concerns about the landscape, about travel, about tourism in America seem today, after almost thirty continued years of the great suburban transformation. One struggles to find the proper words to express the extent to which the New American Landscape has nullified the differences among America's traditionally diverse regions. It has homogenized the style and look of our residential and commercial architecture. It has literally brutalized whatever natural element yet survives. Like an advancing army whose weapons are billboards and

The Myth of Travel

commercial strips, strategic shopping malls, and dazzling suburban office towers, the New American Landscape brazenly, shamelessly erects, ejects, and ejaculates itself upon an exhausted and used-up continent, sweeping away all vestiges of nature, of history, of our collective past.

Our reaction as a people is both indifferent and celebratory. We appear indifferent to the physical and environmental loss of our cultural heritage as authentic small towns and charming countryside are paved over. At the same time we seem pleased and satisfied in having created a physical environment in which it is literally possible to be no more than minutes by car away from a refrigerated soft drink.

As the landscape aesthetically condenses into its lowest common denominator, as geographic and historic diversity disappear, as the very reason to travel becomes less compelling, ours becomes increasingly an age in which everyone seems obsessed with travel. Travel enhances the sale of products and services, animates movie plots, excites romantic relationships, and for the society at large, serves as a cultural model for behavior. We envy. We respect. We admire the savvy traveler. We even grow old to retire . . . and to travel. For all our growing fascination with travel and travelers, with all of the travel guides, travel books, travel videos, travel magazines, and travel sections in the newspapers, one hears precious little about the reality of travel within America. What is that reality? Ironically, the great suburban transformation has remade travel, from one part of the New American Landscape to another, into merely physical motion.

One travels thousands of miles to shop in the same chain stores, eat at the same chain restaurants, and sleep in the same chain motels. Be it Portland, Oregon, or Portland, Maine, pre-

The Myth of Travel

mium malls are well defined by their trendy, upscale boutiques, fern bars, and coffeehouses offering nonfat yogurt and low-cholesterol treats. As the environment becomes a seamless web of advertising hype, as suburban Atlanta becomes indistinguishable from suburban Seattle, one might as well travel with eyes closed. In fact, one might as well not travel at all.

To the metaphoric sensibility, the highway takes us to no more an intriguing place than its own endless ribbon of asphalt and concrete. To the metaphoric sensibility the highway, not the destination, is the destination. Highways do not just take travelers to some particular place. Highways act upon, massage, and transform the distant traveler and the local resident alike, through the experience of the road itself. Forget the usual romantic illusions about traveling the great American road. All such nonsense presupposes that the landscape reflects natural and historic conditions. The New American Landscape is synthetic, ahistorical, and, most decidedly, unnatural.

The experience of the highway, which is the essence of the suburban transformation, is the experience of phony travel—motion without meaning. Movement in your car from one point to another is still real, but travel, the exposure to that which is worth seeing and experiencing, is for the most part an impossible expectation on the American road. Those who travel on today's highways arrive brain dead, their sensibilities a victim of the ordeal of passage. To travel the American highway is to go nowhere one has not already been. To travel the American highway is to simply repeat the visual and visceral exposure to commercialism that has contributed to our wretched aesthetic condition.

The Myth of Travel

Consider with an open mind the following observations about travel in contemporary America and contemporary Americans:

Travel Reality No. 1: *You cannot travel in America without having to endure commercial messages persuading you to buy something.* Billboards and commercial signs accost us in our cars. Commercials and "infotainment" assail us on movie screens in airplanes. The travel experience itself has become just one additional sales channel for advertisers to try to sell something, anything, regardless of its relevance to the traveler's journey. Considering that many people travel to shop, why not shop while traveling?

Travel Reality No. 2: *Travel in America has become an increasingly public experience in the worst sense of the word "public."* For those who have not thought about it, I will explain that *public* has become the dirty word for community. A community is a group of people who share common values and bonds that tie them together. The public is that vast mass of persons who seem to have no common values and bonds that tie them together other than the desire to stick it to the other guy before he sticks it to them.

While all travel by necessity forces the traveler to surrender some privacy, the fact that we share common highways, airplanes, and toilets should not account for the perception that we are cheek-to-jowl in traveling togetherness. The one-size-fits-all concept, so popular in polyester socks, is expanding to absorb us in one classless traveling public mass headed hell-bent for some common destination, with emphasis on the word *common.* Ironically, the more exclusive and first-class travel becomes, as in flying first class, the more pretentious, ostentatious, and farcical such travel seems to be. The un-

The Myth of Travel

avoidable truth is that hundreds of thousands of people cannot physically be moved around the country on a daily basis
without sacrificing too much privacy, comfort, self-respect,
and human dignity to make the whole effort worth the
trouble.

Travel Reality No. 3: *Business travel in America is a nonevent.*
The frequent business traveler would rather not travel, because he or she knows that business travel is unpleasant and
exhausting. There is no glamour, no adventure, no meaning
in traveling for business. Business travel is to travel as masturbation is to sex. No, business travel is to travel as thinking
about masturbation is to sex.

Travel Reality No. 4: *The process of travel itself is supposed to
magically transform the unacceptable into the desirably exotic.* In
the past, one traveled to increase one's knowledge of, and familiarity with, the best some locale had to offer. One traveled
to broaden one's horizons, to experience away from home
that which was worth experiencing had it been possible to do
so at home. Today, when traveling, one is supposed to be interested in seeing people and things one would never dream
of wanting to see at home.

On my first and last ship cruise in the Caribbean, I went
ashore on one of those tropical islands that looks enchanting
from a distance. Sailing closer, I realized the lush tropical
vegetation was hiding from view unkempt, broken-down
shacks and rickety stores. Disembarking on the town dock, I
was confronted by young street urchins with out-stretched
palms accompanied by a pack of barking, snarling dogs. Everywhere, litter and garbage were strewn in all directions as
far as the eye could see. A rusting car with its wheels gone
greeted me and my arriving fellow travelers. A large clap-

The Myth of Travel

board sign with missing letters welcomed visitors to beautiful Tortola, crown jewel of the Caribbean. My traveling com-
panion, a dean of a well-known, leading university, said
something inane about what a pleasant island this was. In
disbelief, I wondered why she paid $2,000 to visit the eco-
nomically disadvantaged when she could have done so at
home for far less.

Travel Reality No. 5: *Travel becomes its own reality.* Travel is
no longer just a means of getting from point A to point B.
Travel has become organized, bureaucratized, institutionalized. Travel is an industry and, for many locations, a major
part of the economy. It is in the economic interests of restau-
rateurs, hotel and resort operators, airlines, travel agents, oil
companies, and countless others to keep us on the road and
in the skies—perpetually. When the National Park Service
came under criticism for its policy at Yellowstone of letting
wildfires burn as a natural component of the ecosystem, the
objections were strictly economic. How will letting fires burn
impact the local tourist business? The agenda of the travel
industry has indelibly changed the way everyone travels,
even the hitchhiker.

Ironically, the New Man is quite at home when traveling
on the New American Landscape. How could he not be? His
every need and whim, his lodging, his food, his need to consume—all are met by familiar vendors whose nationally recognized logos and beloved reputations are as second nature
to him. As today's travelers consume their way through and
across our consumable landscape, they are at once comfortable and at ease. Such familiarity and acceptance of place by
the American traveler are apparent as one encounters our fellows on the ubiquitous highway.

The Myth of Travel

The New Man arrives at his destination of choice not as a respectful guest in someone else's community. He arrives as an expectant consumer, as desirous of timely and attentive service as he would be at home. Encouraged to buy everything in sight, the New Man does not experience his destination so much as forage the landscape in search of a vacation bargain. Not only does the New Man consume those products and services necessary to sustain him physically on his journey, but he quite literally consumes all that he experiences in much the same fashion. On the highway, the New Man is conditioned and encouraged to ignore what might remain of historic continuity and the contextual whole. He deconstructs all before him into discrete components to be speedily sized-up from his moving car. The New American Landscape has become the equivalent of an infinite supermarket shelf. The highway is a never-ending aisle on which we speed by to select a package of Grand Canyon, a jar of WalMart, a bag of Disneyland. Destinations, services, entertainment—all have become fundamentally equal as entities to be consumed.

Travel has become a consumer experience that only incidentally involves physically moving through space. Soon, seeing the video will be superior to actually being in any particular place. Wherever one might go will be essentially the same as wherever one is. Multiculturalism and heterogeneity are praised. However, they are all but negated in the New American Landscape that is a monoculture defined by consumption, convenience, repetition, security, and predictability.

The late Marxist political philosopher Herbert Marcuse, in *One Dimensional Man,* suggested that the American traveler mistakes tourism as a worthy substitute for the real experience of living somewhere. Even acknowledging that travel is no substitute for residence, it becomes necessary to ask how so many millions can travel so many millions of miles and understand so little about the New American Landscape. The answer is that people do not travel to understand what they experience. For many of today's travelers, the decidedly synthetic experience of traveling itself is far more enticing than the actual experience of any particular destination. Certainly the New Man does not travel to experience some different and unfamiliar environment. The New Man does not even travel to experience the New American Landscape, because as a child of suburbia, he intuitively knows its familiar and predictable character. Rather, armed with the same bargaining skills of any wily consumer steeped in the protocol of consumption, the New Man travels to be solicited by vendors great and small.

The New Man imposes himself on the environment, first physically by his quite obvious presence (car, camper van, boat trailer, videocam, screaming kids, barking dogs) and then demographically, by conditioning sales-savvy vendors to cater to his tastes. Thus, the New Man becomes an unconscious proselytizer for himself and the millions like him who buy the Winnebagos, eat the fast-food slop, sleep in the noisy motel chains, and admire the billboards.

Across the New American Landscape travel millions whose aim is to purchase what they believe they cannot purchase at home. Beyond goods and services, and gifts to take back to family and friends, today's New Man travels to purchase a cure for whatever sense of inadequacy he may have regarding social performance. He travels to be perceived as connected

The Myth of Travel

to all the cultural icons to which we so faithfully subscribe. Above all, like his historic predecessors, real or imagined by Hollywood, he travels to find himself.

The pathetic irony is that today's New Man, out there on the highway as the focal point for powerful enticements to consume, has indeed found himself. Trouble is, he has found the rest of us, and whether we like it or not, he has changed how we too must travel on the New American Landscape. In the mystique and technique of travel, the New Man seeks to perfect himself. The greater his motion, the greater his chance of attaining perfection. So it is no surprise that the New American Landscape, designed to facilitate perfection, is itself in perpetual existential motion, ever redefining necessary modalities of seduction and anesthetization.

Travel in America promises adventure and novelty while delivering standardization and mediocrity. Travel is not an escape from the ugliness around us but a principal agent in creating and sustaining our wretched aesthetic condition.

5 THE AESTHETICS OF THE NEW MAN
Beauty R Us

Why is it that Americans are more comfortable talking about their intimate sexual life than they are talking about art? The obvious answer is that almost everybody knows something about sex, but few know anything about art. Fewer still know anything about aesthetics. In the world's most wealthy consumer society, capable and successful people break out in a cold sweat at the prospect of discussing art.

Is it not curious that for the better part of the last ninety years, Americans have received art instruction in their public schools? This art instruction was not an elective but a required course in the primary education curriculum. Is it not even more curious still that attendance at art museums and art galleries during any given year is measured in the millions? On a more mundane but fundamental level, billions of dollars have been spent decorating, redecorating, upgrading and "improving" the American home. Yet for all of this exposure to "art" and "improvement," America is a country in which bad taste has become a birthright—institutionalized and incorporated into the landscape.

What would have happened if we had spent billions over

the better part of a century to educate and instruct in mathematics, language, business, or mechanical arts and suffered the same dismal results? We would witness accusations and allegations of incompetence, fraud, criminal conduct, and worse. A collective national indignation would cry out for corrective measures, new programs, and finally, sought-after results. Such is the scenario now unfolding concerning the apparent demise of general literacy. However, in the realm of aesthetics, in the peculiar and bizarre world of art education, apparently millions can be spent with no one held accountable for the results.

As subjects to be studied and appreciated, art and beauty have been inadequately presented to Americans. While elementary school students may enthusiastically soil themselves with finger paints, their playful experience of art suggests that it is not a subject worthy of serious consideration. As a people, Americans have failed to emotionally experience aesthetics much beyond grade school, for it is not long before the finger paints are put away, and we are not again likely to be told that playful and joyous aesthetic experiences have value.

Though therapeutic values have instructed us how to relate emotionally to the world with our inner selves, we have not been taught to deal with aesthetics emotionally. Americans' aesthetic preferences have been more a function of their social class identities and the homogenizing influence of the New American Landscape than of any genuine emotional experience of art or beauty. Why have we as a people—as compared to the French, the Italians, and others—never practiced and celebrated art and the beauty of nature as an emotional experience? Why for us have art and aesthetics been at best intellectual abstractions and at worst social pretensions?

The explanations are varied. The American sensibility dating back to the eighteenth century has been ambivalent about the value of beauty and art. Patrons of the arts were usually wealthy and elite. They aroused opposition from the common man and from those religious quarters that considered art a blasphemous idolatry. Remember the Puritans, whose sense of self-denial, deferment of gratification, and professed obligation to God and community surely must comprise the ultimate horror for today's New Man. However, more fundamentally, the American character has been best understood as pragmatic and utilitarian. The practical individuals of the frontier were people of commerce and industry. They represented an America entering the industrial age with an innate sense that whatever beauty might exist, especially in the man-made world, followed form and function. Beauty had value only in some vague and peripheral way.

In the early days of the conservation movement, spectacular scenery was considered of value for its spectacle alone. Scenery motivated enthusiasts to work diligently for the preservation of such awe-inspiring landscapes as Yellowstone and Yosemite. However, in a peculiarly American way, even scenery had to pass some kind of pragmatic test. Everyday, ordinary scenery would not justify the concern of preservationists. By definition, only the most spectacular scenery, the scenery that lent itself to superlatives (the biggest, the highest, the deepest, the hottest, and so on) deserved the support of conservationists. A landscape so spectacular, so superlative, needed to be preserved as a matter of good old-fashioned common sense; even otherwise exploitative, entrepreneurial, Darwin enthusiasts could understand that.

Demanding that scenery meet the test of pragmatism impeded American aesthetic sensibilities. In addition, our tradition of male supremacy discredited appreciation of natural beauty as unmanly and feminine. Real men were not to worry about such ethereal and ephemeral concerns as natural beauty, not when the nation called out for more railroads, canals, steel mills, munitions factories, and steamships. Real men needed to direct their energies and intellects toward the realization of America's industrial destiny. Scenic beauty would be left to women and would be considered by men, and consequently by society at large, no more seriously than any other concern relegated to the domain of feminine responsibility. Regrettably, understanding and appreciating the beauty of nature and the beauty of art was considered far less important than making money, making war, and making love.

Speculation concerning the historic causes of our wretched aesthetic condition can be an exhausting and fruitless exercise. Fundamentally, there is no denying the enormity of bad taste and bad aesthetic judgment that is evident throughout American society. There is no ugliness like the ugliness of poverty. However, the ugliness of the nouveau riche, ensconced in their pretentious houses and inflicting on their fellows excessive and ostentatious behavior, is particularly inexcusable. This is especially true given the education and incomes of the perpetrators of such questionable and tasteless excess.

Paul Fussell in his amusing book *Class* drew a telling portrait of American taste as it is manifested among our various social classes. That Americans of all social classes share certain aesthetic values should come as no surprise to those who understand the homogenizing influence, not only of the mass media, but of the New American Landscape itself.

Let us consider what I would call an aesthetic profile of the New Man.

1. *Bigger is better.* In the finest American tradition, the New Man instinctively believes that if something is good, axiomatically, a larger-size version will be so much the better. Hence, the bigger the suburban tract house, the better. The bigger the pickup truck, the better. The bigger a woman's breasts, the better. Of course, such giganticism is reflected in commercial and public buildings and in the very endless and infinitely expanding character of the New American Landscape itself.

2. *More is better than less.* A corollary to bigger is better. More is better than less is reflected in the apparent necessity to overwhelm the visual sense with images of the infinite. This numerical excess is witnessed every Christmas in countless neighborhoods in which residents compete for attention by having more outdoor Christmas lights than their neighbors. Inside the home, empty wall and floor space is considered by the typical American to constitute an aesthetic crime that can only be rectified by immediately filling said empty space with something—anything.

3. *The obvious is always superior to the subtle.* In the dead of night, when all the world should be fast asleep, Americans awake in a cold sweat and wonder if people notice them. So too in their waking hours, our fellows ponder to what extent they, in their choice of wardrobe, selection of automobile, and commitment to a particular home style, are receiv-

Aesthetics of the New Man

ing the attention, the notice, the appreciation that they deserve from friends and neighbors.

To assure that he is not somehow being overlooked, the New Man will invariably paint his home in the most intense color. He will festoon the rear of his car with stickers and decals disclosing where he went to school. He will exhibit his affiliation with the local public television station (in many communities the definition of membership in the intellectual class) and reveal that he loves his dog. Of course, he will inevitably illuminate the outside of his house with light bulbs powerful enough to provide security at the state prison. Ring the doorbell and you will hear, not the subdued call of a comforting chime, but a mind-numbing buzz, equaled only by the gut-wrenching alarm of his bedside clock. For after all, the New Man must not gently rise but must startle himself awake, least he miss entirely the point of getting out of bed.

4. *Louder is better.* While many might protest that it is a golden silence for which they long, Americans seem increasingly fascinated with those appliances and devices that generate the most noise. Certainly the popularity of what has come to be the ubiquitous leaf blower (particularly the ultraloud gasoline-powered version) is not due entirely to its utility, of which observers have noted little. Much of its popularity is due to the raw machismo and riveting phallic power such weapons of backyard domesticity bestow.

To the incessant whine of the leaf blower we must add the primordial beat of car stereos, shattering neighborhood tranquillity at all hours of the day and night. Let us not forget the increasing proliferation of barking dogs and the apparent necessity of dog owners to leave their animals outside to howl and squeal at will, regardless of how disturbing to others. Silence is an important component of aesthetics and one of the first of its attributes to be sacrificed in the name of expediency.

5. *The inappropriate is usually preferable to the appropriate.* Americans think nothing of erecting colonial Georgian houses in the deserts of Arizona, of building white-pillared southern plantations in the mountains of the Pacific northwest, of choosing to live in something called a Mediterranean-style home thousands of miles from the Mediterranean Sea. As we have explained, the New American Landscape cannot tolerate an authentic sense of history and of genuine local identity. The construction of English and French chalets on the plains of Kansas affirms the elasticity and plasticity of a landscape and an aesthetic sense that does not grasp, in any meaningful way, the notion of appropriate design.

Now, such characterizations of the American public can be considered sources of amusement. Far from amusing, my aesthetic profile proves that art and the appreciation of beauty have failed to be seriously understood by the New Man. He embodies the aesthetics of mimesis and immanence as defined by his own naked appetite.

There will be those who ask: so what? Those who would contend that the majority has never understood art and never exercised any meaningful aesthetic judgment. While that is undeniably true, such responses miss the point. For the first time in history, it is not the members of some elite minority—such as old money, intellectuals, or artists—but the new men of the New American Landscape, the majority, who are setting the aesthetic standards. Most important, these new men are setting standards not just for themselves but for the entire society at large. The New Man is redefining society's

Aesthetics of the New Man

aesthetic standards at the very time that art has failed to emotionally engage the New Man.

6. *Art and aesthetic values are an intolerable abstraction.*
Those new men who live on the New American Landscape
respond to emotive myths that resonate in their lives, infus-
ing their pathetic existence with meaning. The myth of travel
and the myth of therapy are clearly grasped and understood.
The New Man will not tolerate abstractions because he can
only understand the concrete and the literal. Art and aesthetic values, as they have been traditionally presented, have
proven an impossibility for current sensibilities to apprehend
and comprehend. This is true, if for no other reason than the
fact that art bores the vast majority of Americans.

7. *Art and the appreciation of aesthetic values are forms of
work.* Americans today work at improving themselves. They
need to work at art to understand it, so they expend energy
visiting museums, attending the symphony and the opera,
and reading "important" books. After a hard day at the office,
relaxing means watching television and reading cheap nov-
els. Experiencing serious art is not how Americans relax, and
how they "relax" is the most significant measure of what is
important and what is not on the New American Landscape.

8. *Art and aesthetic values are mysterious.* Though art is apparently taught in elementary school by friendly, outgoing,
accessible elementary school teachers, art for most Americans
and for those of all social classes is anything but friendly and
accessible. Of all the subjects taught in the American school,
art and notions of scenic beauty are not only the most
quickly forgotten, they are the most easily misunderstood.
The meaning of art is unclear and the relevance of art and
aesthetics to Americans is particularly uncertain. The great-

est certainty our fellows share about art is its irrelevancy to their lives.

9. *Art and notions of the beautiful are incredible.* For the New Man, art is incredible, meaning that unlike money, power, romance, crime, and consumer goods, art has no credibility in everyday life. Art and notions of what constitutes beauty apparently have value only to a select few who are seen to use their alleged knowledge and understanding of art and aesthetics as an excuse to feel superior to the common man. On the New American Landscape, art and beauty are, at best, incomprehensible and irrelevant. At worst, art is considered a device with which snobs berate the masses.

For these and other reasons, Americans simply are not, and have not been, interested in art and beauty the way we are interested in sports, shopping, sex, and television personalities. Visitation to art museums notwithstanding, art and aesthetic values are not of interest to the vast majority. Art as it has been packaged, promoted, and presented to the public over the better part of the twentieth century has been a bust. This means that Americans share no conscious common aesthetic sense or experience—the way they share an understanding of sports, movies, and fast food—that unites disparate classes and subcultures in a common bond.

The common American aesthetic experience is aesthetics by default. The aesthetic dimension of the New American Landscape exists to orchestrate and facilitate increased levels of consumption. That most Americans are unconscious of the aesthetics of the great suburban transformation should come as no surprise to those who consider Americans unconscious of numerous aspects of their existence.

But what about the artists themselves, particularly those in

Aesthetics of the New Man

the visual arts. It may be possible to argue that art teachers and educators, and even art critics, have failed to grasp that our society is undergoing a historic aesthetic transformation. However, surely the visual artists themselves must understand the immense real and potential power of the landscape to create a new aesthetic dimension in the lives of Americans. Given the interpretative capabilities of artists, one would expect some recognition, some insight from the art world regarding the real meaning of the great suburban transformation.

I must confess my disappointment in being unable to detect any such acknowledgment from the professional artist. Yet that should come as no surprise to those who have long understood that the visual arts are by now oblivious to all but their own narrow concerns. For years the visual arts have failed to perform perhaps the single most significant function the artist can offer—that is, to explain, to portray, to impart meaning to that which the common man is otherwise unable to understand.

Artists, because of their innate ability to comprehend subtle changes taking place in the world around them, are especially suited, and one could argue morally obligated, to inform us through works of art of the nature of the times. Yet one is hard-pressed to point to any significant work of visual art or to any significant artists who have made clear the real meaning of the great suburban transformation. Rather than aloof and immune from the conventional wisdom, as artists ironically fancy themselves, visual artists have fallen victim to each of the conventions that define life on the New American Landscape. Art has degenerated into self-serving therapeutic validation of the narcissistic sensibility and, in so do-

Aesthetics of the New Man

ing, has failed to paint a true picture of either our exterior or interior ugliness.

For the New Man, the aesthetics of the New American Landscape are momentary, remaining viable and worthy of acknowledgment only for as long as desire is satisfied. The New Man, hungering for meaning in an increasingly meaningless environment, possesses the raw emotional capability to respond to an aesthetic appeal that defines beauty not as an abstraction but as an emotional reality. Given the historical failure of art and aesthetic values to have any significant meaning in American life, the operative question continues to be: How can we emotionally engage the New Man and turn aesthetics into a gut-wrenching reality out there on the mean streets of the great suburban transformation?

Clearly, a new American aesthetic sense calls out to be defined and made real to the New Man. Let us clarify our meaning. Over time, aesthetics can unite and reanimate an environmental agenda, even an agenda balkanized into numerous divergent, and competing, issues. Playing the aesthetic card in a way it has not been played before communicates through a cathartic aesthetic experience that transcendence of self-absorption is possible. Such a notion is a truly self-liberating one whose significance should not be overlooked by a population restless, agitated, and hungering for something real.

6 BILLBOARDS
Dominant Visual Modality
of the New American Landscape

A s we have seen, educators, critics, and artists have failed to imbue Americans with a common sense of aesthetics, succeeding only in privatizing, mystifying, and abstracting the aesthetic impulse. As a society, we have been both unable and unwilling to respond to the obtuse and belabored instruction in the arts of our aesthetic betters. Historically, we have turned our collective backs in disinterest and distrust.

At the same time, Americans have been aesthetically engaged more adroitly by the mass media and national retailers. Through emotionally charged advertising and retail design, the manufacturers and distributors of consumer products have created a de facto aesthetic standard. To an increasingly comprehensive degree, it defines the look and feel of the New American Landscape.

There are numerous candidates among American business whose contribution to our wretched aesthetic condition is deserving of scrutiny. However, none has gone further in its ability to undermine traditional notions of aesthetics and to bend and shape our de facto national aesthetic to its purposes than the outdoor advertising industry, as it likes to be called.

Of all the players appealing to the debased sensibilities of the New Man, none is more capable, more calculating, more nefarious, and more successful than the billboard industry. It has succeeded in corrupting and tainting public aesthetics, public welfare, and public consciousness. Billboards are intrusive, obnoxious, annoying, and, unlike television, they cannot be turned off.

"Billboard advertising is good for America," claims a billboard company spokesperson expressing opposition to proposed regulation of billboards.

"You can't impose your subjective values regarding what is aesthetic on the community at large," asserts a billboard company executive declaring that aesthetic standards are subjective and billboard opponents elitists.

"So what if we cut down a few trees. I don't understand why that's such a big deal." So says a billboard company representative reacting with surprise at San Jose, California, citizens outraged over his company cutting down a grove of eucalyptus trees on public land that happened to be blocking motorists' view of billboards from the highway.

During the 1980s the billboard lobby attempted and in some cases succeeded in incorporating the following civic-minded notions into law:

— Change the purpose of the Highway Beautification Act from protecting scenic beauty to preserving "communications through the outdoor medium."
— Abolish the traditional use of local municipal authority to remove billboards.
— Require that all trees blocking a billboard would by law be cut down at taxpayer expense.

A profile of the billboard industry reveals more than the inner workings of a lawful business whose activities and purposes border on the criminal. It reveals just how susceptible we have become to the corrupting influences, not of the truly powerful, but ironically of the simply persistent and incalculably clever. To put things in perspective, consider that the tobacco industry recorded annual sales in 1991 of approximately $32 billion, while the billboard industry grossed only $1.4 billion in 1989. Nationwide the billboard industry employs fewer than 13,000 people. Yet the billboard industry sets the aesthetic standards that have come to define America.

Billboards are like telephone poles. Literally no one in America, perhaps not even the billboard industry itself, knows how many billboards exist. To circumvent regulation, the Outdoor Advertising Association of America (OAAA), which lobbies on behalf of the billboard industry, has historically opposed legislation requiring official billboard counts. Nevertheless, the Federal Highway Administration (FHA) occasionally attempts an estimate. In 1986 the FHA identified Kentucky as having more billboards than any other state—a total of 51,635 on federal highways alone. Florida weighed in with 30,000 and California with more than 15,000. While many agree there are at least 500,000 billboards visually polluting the nation's commercial, rural, and residential areas, some knowledgeable observers put the figure much higher.

The billboard industry likes to point out that the public is not as aware of billboards as it used to be. The implication is that there are fewer billboards today than in the past. In reality the public fails to notice billboards as much today as in the past—although not necessarily because billboards are fewer, smaller, or generally less visually intrusive. The public

Billboards

"sees" fewer billboards today because billboards are now competing for public attention, not just with other billboards or other retail advertising signs but with the entire landscape itself. The general level of commercialism within and throughout the environment is so much more intense than it was just twenty-five years ago that we do not notice individual billboards the way we once did.

While the public may be less conscious of billboards, the ubiquitous billboard continues to be one of the most successful, and perhaps the most profitable, advertising media in our advertising-saturated consumer society. Two factors account for the billboard industry's profitability. The first is technological. Compared to the cost of the equipment required to broadcast a radio or television program, write, print, and distribute a newspaper or magazine, the cost of physically erecting a billboard is quite low.

More interesting from a public policy perspective is the fact that billboard companies pay almost nothing to maintain the cost of the public right-of-way, without which privately owned billboards have no value. In San Francisco billboards that gross as much as $60,000 annually pay the city only $26 in yearly tax revenue. Make no mistake, that's $26. Billboard companies pay neither road use taxes nor fees specifically earmarked for highway maintenance, even though they use the public highways to do business. The billboard industry's costs are insignificant compared to its competitors. Low costs translate into low advertising rates.

Advertisers of consumer products know that advertising via billboards is considerably less expensive than television, radio, newspapers, magazines, and direct mail. For the tobacco industry and distributors of hard liquor, prevented by law and voluntary agreement from using radio and television, billboards are considered to be a particularly cost-effective means of reaching the intended audience. Billboard advertisers are willing to bet that billboards will have an impact on consumers, subconsciously if not consciously. As advertisers see it, the low cost of advertising on a billboard is worth the acceptable risk of a billboard failing to register on the conscious mind of the speeding motorist. If not this trip down the highway, perhaps the next drive by will result in recognition of the billboard's enticing message.

Low costs translate into low rates for advertisers and big profits to billboard companies. What has the billboard industry done with its immense profits since the 1960s? First, the outdoor advertising industry has been one of America's most generous political contributors. Campaign contributions, honoraria, and free billboard space have all been generously given to candidates for local, state, and national office. Ironically, some of Washington's most enthusiastic supporters of environmental legislation have been recipients of billboard industry PAC contributions, including Mr. Environment himself, former senator and now vice president, Al Gore.

Between 1983 and 1988 the billboard lobby, under the direction of now-retired OAAA executive director Vernon Clark, paid members of Congress over $640,000 in honoraria. This is the now-illegal practice of giving money to members of Congress for their personal use in return for speeches and presentations. The billboard industry's generosity exceeded that of all other industries except tobacco and defense. Under pressure to discontinue the outrageous practice of selling favors, Congress discontinued the dishonorable honoraria. For a complete analysis of the impact of the billboard industry's financial contributions on Capitol Hill, see *The Best Congress Money Can Buy,* by Philip Stern.

As recently as the late 1950s, the billboard industry was comprised of small, locally owned and operated billboard companies. Many were in and out of trouble with local authorities, perpetually in danger of their billboards being taken down in violation of local nuisance ordinances. It was a decade in which the television industry, then not even ten years old, was already grossing hundreds of millions of dollars annually from commercials. The much-older billboard industry was hanging on in an advertising backwater, with gross revenues dwarfed not only by television but by radio, newspapers, and magazines.

How did billboards, in the 1950s a small-time business with a tacky, low-class reputation as an also-ran in the advertising game, reemerge in the 1960s as a contender for big advertising dollars? Do not be surprised to discover that the billboard industry used federal billboard control legislation as the means to rejuvenate itself. Such a paradox evolved undetected by, and beyond the understanding of, the proponents of billboard reform.

It did not require genius to realize that the about-to-be constructed interstate highway system, whose enabling legislation was enacted in 1956 and whose completion was not anticipated until the 1970s, would revolutionize the way Americans traveled, commuted, and spent their money. Most of all it would change the way they defined themselves. Even the fast-buck artists in the billboard business understood that the interstates would sharply concentrate and focus a new audience for billboards, presenting incredible opportunities to expand and "upgrade" outdoor advertising.

Guaranteeing a place for billboards on the interstate system required the billboard industry to present a united front against the industry's longtime foes: the advocates of billboard control. The billboard companies orchestrated their scheme through the OAAA, which began lobbying Congress for favorable treatment, claiming that billboards were "good for business." Billboard interests contended that those who called for restrictions or for an end to billboards were, at best, kooky little old ladies from the local garden club. At worst, billboard critics were said to be card-carrying Communists out to destroy the American way of life.

Washington had seen powerful industry lobbyists attempt to forestall government regulation before, but the nation's capital had not seen anything like the OAAA and Vernon Clark, the key strategist of the powerful billboard lobby on Capitol Hill. Clark was a clever and cunning leader. He convinced the companies he represented to support, not oppose, the Highway Beautification Act (HBA), first proposed in 1964 by the Johnson administration as a means for federal control of billboards on federally funded highways.

The HBA further established the federal government's claim, first advocated in the 1950s, that it could broadly regulate the establishment of billboards adjacent to both the new interstate and the primary federal highway system. However, the legislation also legitimized the billboard industry in two important ways. First, it did not ban new billboards or require the total removal of existing billboards. Consequently, it codified in law an undefined but, one could argue, implied right of billboards to exist in some fashion, as far as the federal government was concerned.

Furthermore, the HBA mandated that if the law required

Billboards

the removal of any existing billboards, as it did in rural areas, that billboard companies would be paid off in cash—"compensated," as the billboard industry prefers to phrase it. This money was to be allocated jointly by Congress and the states. Vernon Clark shrewdly suspected what few others were able to foresee: the political inability of the Congress to allocate the millions of dollars necessary to pay off the billboard companies for removal of billboards along rural federal highways.

Since the enactment of the HBA in 1965, the federal government has paid the billboard companies approximately $225 million to take down an estimated 14,000 billboards. The projected cost to remove those additional billboards still in violation of the HBA is about $2 billion. At the historical rate of congressional allocation of billboard removal funds, it will take another 1,000 years to finish the job.

Clark calculated, quite accurately as history proved, that after the first few years of inadequately funding the billboard company enrichment program, Congress would bail out. Congress's failure to follow through left the Highway Beautification Act a toothless regulator of the billboard industry. In recent years billboard removal funds have been only sporadically allocated. In 1990 only 226 billboards were removed, according to the Federal Highway Administration. At the same time, tens of thousands of new, larger billboards have continued to go up in areas not covered by the lax standards of the HBA.

In addition, the HBA established both the industry's legitimacy and the nefarious concept that billboard polluters could continue polluting unless they were handsomely paid to stop. So, the billboard lobby had it both ways. Existing billboards would be permitted to continue standing, or the billboard companies would be paid cash to have them removed.

Fine print in the HBA revealed that the billboard companies would be able to determine which billboards were to be taken down and influence the amount of money to be paid. The billboard companies selected billboards for removal in locations that were not profitable, billboards they had scheduled to be removed anyway. Compensation turned out to be, not the cost to physically remove a billboard, but a percentage of the amount of money a billboard would earn if left standing for several years. This meant that for the removal of one billboard, a billboard company might receive hundreds of thousands of taxpayer dollars.

Ironically, while the HBA forced taxpayers to pay the billboard industry to stop polluting in some locations, it allowed billboard companies to start polluting in thousands of new areas. The legislation permitted that new billboards could be erected along the interstates and primary highways in locations zoned as industrial or commercial or considered to be unzoned commercial or industrial areas. The actual definition of what constituted an industrial or commercial zone was reserved, not for the federal or state governments to decide, but for local jurisdictions to evaluate. Literally thousands of local municipalities particularly susceptible to high-pressure lobbying by the billboard industry were permitted under the federal law to zone essentially empty fields adjacent to interstates as commercial or industrial areas, and they did so. The practice, called "phony zoning," continues to this day. The unzoned commercial area loophole in the HBA has allowed billboards to go up next to railroad tracks, country stores, even farmhouses, because farms or home businesses are considered a commercial enterprise.

With taxpayer-supplied money, the industry then erected new and bigger billboards, many within less than a mile of the site of a billboard the government had previously paid a billboard company to remove. In 1983 the federal government paid for the removal of 2,235 billboards while the same year the billboard industry put up 13,522 new billboards. The Congressional Research Service estimates that almost 50,000 new billboards were erected between 1986 and 1988. Since the passage of the HBA, the billboard industry has legally erected over 320,000 new billboards, and more continue to go up even as you read this.

States and communities eager to have existing billboards taken down under the HBA and realizing that federal money would not be allocated enacted local ordinances requiring that the billboards be removed. The industry responded in 1978 by pressuring Congress to amend the HBA to prevent local ordinances from mandating removal of existing billboards without the payment of cash. In other words, the cash payment provision of the federal legislation, by act of Congress, was required of all local billboard removal ordinances affecting federal highways. To this day, local governments must spend taxpayer dollars to pay off billboard companies to remove existing billboards on federal highways in their communities. It is improbable that such funding will ever be adequately provided by local governments, which of course was the notion motivating the billboard lobby's passage of the amendment.

Unbelievably, the Highway Beautification Act sets no meaningful standards regarding the size or height of billboards or the distance between billboards. After the act's passage in 1965, the powerful billboard industry successfully lobbied for subsequent amendments that further weakened the already anemic billboard control legislation. No more pernicious example can be found than a decision in the early years of the Reagan administration permitting individual states to allow billboard companies to legally cut down trees and other vegetation on public land blocking motorists' views of billboards on private land. Currently twenty-four states—including the supposedly environmentally conscious state of California— allow the clear-cutting of public trees and landscaping to enhance the visibility and value of privately owned billboards. In some states, state highway departments cut down trees on behalf of billboard companies petitioning for what the industry calls "visibility improvement." Knowledgeable observers estimate that millions of trees on public lands have been destroyed, and the practice continues to this day. For a comprehensive history of federal billboard control legislation and an in-depth analysis of the HBA, see *Billboards: The Environmental Movement's Greatest Failure,* by Charles Floyd.

The public pays for the streets and highways next to which billboards are erected, continues to pay for road maintenance, and finally is forced to be a captive audience for commercial messages. The notion that the public should pay billboard companies to remove billboards, whose value is solely due to their ability to be seen from the public right of way, is patently absurd. The billboard companies have no right to appropriate a public investment for their own financial gain. Even this short litany of excesses by the billboard industry demonstrates that the industry is adept at buying elected officials. It is capable of manipulating legislation and acting solely in its own interests, no matter how great the aesthetic cost or how much money it succeeds in extorting from the public.

As the U.S. Supreme Court and other federal and state courts have consistently ruled, billboards are a private, parasitic use of a public investment. The courts have affirmed the public's legitimate right to regulate, and even prohibit, billboards. These decisions are based in part on the landmark 1954 zoning case of *Berman v. Parker.* In the *Berman* decision, Justice William O. Douglas observed that "the concept of public welfare is broad and inclusive. . . . The values it represents are spiritual as well as physical, aesthetic as well as monetary. It is within the power of the legislature to determine that the community should be beautiful as well as healthy, spacious as well as clean." In a 1984 decision, *Taxpayers for Vincent v. the City of Los Angeles,* the U.S. Supreme Court ruled, "municipalities have a weighty, essentially aesthetic interest in proscribing intrusive and unpleasant formats for expression." The failure of the Highway Beautification Act and other billboard control legislation is quite simply a failure of political will.

How have we permitted a tiny nickel-and-dime industry that manufactures no socially redeeming product or service; employs a decreasing number of low-wage, low-tech personnel who are increasingly being replaced by automation; exists on public subsidies that it spends to corrupt the legislative process; ties up the courts in frivolous litigation solely to intimidate attempts to ban new billboards at the local level; and advertises tobacco and alcohol, especially in minority neighborhoods, to destroy the landscape of the entire nation? The answers are not pleasant to contemplate. Either the public cannot see the aesthetic destruction caused by billboard proliferation, or it does not care. In all likelihood, the public by now is anesthetized to the manipulative purposes of the New American Landscape.

The pathology of the New American Landscape is in inverse proportion to the health and prosperity of the billboard industry. In the 1980s, as the industry proceeded to turn the Highway Beautification Act into the "Outdoor Advertising Subsidy Act," only one tiny and almost unknown organization attempted to alert an unknowing public. The story of Scenic America and its heroic efforts to bring down the wrath of public indignation on the sleazy goings-on of the billboard lobby and its congressional apologists needs to be told.

This story is worth telling not because Scenic America succeeded in doing something about billboards—it did not. The failure of Scenic America to derail the steamroller of billboard proliferation is the story of a small cadre of mostly rich, upper middle-class, white elitists and their total and fundamental inability, not only to politically defeat the billboard industry but to conceptually grasp the real meaning of billboard proliferation. Scenic America's members were unable to understand that billboards are not an isolated political phenomenon but the tip of a social and cultural iceberg. They failed to comprehend that billboards define the seductive and compelling liturgical function of the New American Landscape. This is a metaphor for the final defeat of WASP elitism by the crude and bestial sensibilities of the New Man.

Since the beginning, the organized opposition to billboards has consisted largely of wealthy, socially connected, old-money types. Such people saw the need to clean up billboard blight as just another example of the necessity for political reform and good government. In the tradition of progressive Republicanism, as typified by Theodore Roosevelt and later Thomas Dewey, many very wealthy, civic-minded individuals lent their names, their time, and their money to putting upstart billboard companies in their place—preferably on the way out of town after a visit by the local sheriff. Lawrence Rockefeller was one such upper-class champion of scenic beauty and billboard-free highways.

A number of organizations, quaintly named roadside councils, were formed by enthusiastic billboard-control proponents. The Garden Club of America emerged in the 1950s and early 1960s as the single national organization most active in the fight to do something about billboards. Marion Fuller Brown was Garden Club national vice president, member of the Maine state legislature, and later active on President Jimmy Carter's advisory board on the status of the Highway Beautification Act. She typified the industry's most dedicated opponents: gracious, thoughtful, high-minded, and polite.

In the 1960s, Fuller Brown led the legislative fight in Maine to purchase all existing billboards and prohibit the erection of new ones. Her genteel brethren in the garden clubs were best described as ladies and gentlemen of leisure, unaccustomed to political confrontation and controversy. Well-meaning innocents, they were totally unprepared to compete with bare-knuckled, street-fighting lobbyists like Vernon Clark of the billboard lobby. Clark and his paid-for congressional supporters were determined to co-opt the drafting of the Highway Beautification Act. They deceived even politically savvy Lady Bird Johnson and the act's naive supporters into believing the industry was being cooperative.

With the passage in 1965 of the tainted and industry-influenced Highway Beautification Act, mainstream environmentalists breathed a sigh of relief. The environmental community believed it would never again have to deal with little old ladies from the Garden Club talking about roadside beautification. However, in the 1970s it became clear to knowledgeable observers that the HBA was tragically flawed and had failed to curb billboard pollution. Appeals were made to the Sierra Club and other environmental organizations to take up the issue, but without success. Finally, in the early days of the Reagan administration, a handful of billboard control proponents formed what was soon to become Scenic America. A new organization dedicated to putting teeth into the toothless Highway Beautification Act was born.

It is instructive to note the identities of Scenic America's founders and early supporters. The organization's major strength was also a fundamental weakness—that is, a membership composed of many of the same people who had lost the battle with the industry over the HBA. Lady Bird Johnson retired from the billboard wars content to campaign from her Texas ranch for the planting of wildflowers along highways. Rockefeller foundation money funded the new organization. Marion Fuller Brown brought Garden Club support and members. Retired college professor Yale Maxon, founder of the California Roadside Council, and Ross Netherton, a former official with the Virginia Highway Department, both defeated veterans of the billboard wars, were instrumental in the new organization. An undeniable fixation with past methods and strategies in dealing with the billboard industry blinded many of these longtime billboard reformers to two fundamental realities: (1) they had lost, not won, the battle of the Highway Beautification Act; and (2) the billboard industry was much more powerful and more sophisticated than ever.

Of course, others who had not been involved in the struggle to pass the Highway Beautification Act became prominent leaders in Scenic America. They included Charles Floyd of the University of Georgia, quite possibly the foremost authority on the technical aspects of the HBA. Also involved was Rick Middleton, an articulate Yale graduate and attorney with the Sierra Club Legal Defense Fund. Middleton, one of the few professional environmentalists interested in billboard control, was later to become the director of the Southern Environmental Law Center.

Carroll Shaddock, another graduate of Yale and a well-connected Houston corporate attorney close to influential persons in the Republican party, and Louise Dunlap, a Washington-based environmental lobbyist, also became part of Scenic America's executive committee. Due to my growing interest in the billboard issue, I too found myself a member of the inner circle of policymakers.

If one person can be singled out for special recognition, it is Ed McMahon (no relation to Johnny Carson's former sidekick), who left his law professorship at Georgetown to become Scenic America's first paid executive director and later president. Many in the organization were obviously dedicated to billboard reform. McMahon's passion to clean up billboard blight and curb the excesses of an industry he characterized as possessing an "intent to destroy the scenic heritage of America" approached heroic proportions. During his many years at the helm of this tiny organization, McMahon spent fourteen-hour days fund-raising, lobbying, courting the endorsement of the press. He made fire-breathing speeches on the evil of billboard pollution to civic associations, environmentalists, professional planners, and business groups across the country. He was eventually interviewed on ABC's *Prime Time* and *Good Morning America* and the nightly news on NBC and CBS. McMahon taxed both his health and his marriage with the stress of battling the billboard lobby.

It was McMahon who broadened the attack on billboards beyond the obvious contention that they were destroying the aesthetics of America. He argued that billboards were bad—not good—for business, lowering property values and threatening the popularity of tourist attractions. McMahon formed an allegiance with antismoking activists by educating them to the role billboards played in encouraging the use of cigarettes.

In a brilliant move to reach for support among minorities, McMahon was among the first to point out that billboard companies were systematically targeting African-American neighborhoods with billboards advertising tobacco and liquor. McMahon explained that during the first nine months of 1986, liquor advertisers spent nearly sixteen times as much on billboards directed at African-Americans as they spent on advertising to the general public. A 1987 survey in Saint Louis found that almost 60 percent of the billboards in African-American neighborhoods advertised cigarettes and alcoholic beverages. Such targeting of minorities continues to this day.

In 1986 Scenic America succeeded in getting dramatic and long-overdue billboard reforms through the Senate Public Works Committee. By an eleven-to-four vote that surprised an over-confident billboard lobby, the committee endorsed a permanent ban on all new billboards on federal highways. The committee voted to stop destroying trees on public lands for "visibility improvement" and eliminated all federal cash payments to billboard companies. In addition the committee recognized that local communities, not the federal government, should regulate the removal of billboards.

Awakened by the stinging success of Scenic America's lobbying efforts, the billboard industry was not to be lax again. In a vote of the entire Senate, it soundly defeated the same set of billboard reforms. The industry went on in succeeding years to defeat similar reform legislation orchestrated by Scenic America, including the aptly named Visual Pollution Control Act of 1991, sponsored by Senators John Chafee (a Republican from Rhode Island) and Lloyd Bentsen (a Democrat from Texas). Never again were the proponents of billboard control as close to enacting serious billboard reforms as they had been in the fall of 1986.

The failure of Scenic America symbolizes the failure of the old order and the old mentality to comprehend and deal with the zeitgeist of the New Man. The leaders of Scenic America were politically and legally astute, as only those can be who grow up and make their living in the public sector, academia, and law. They viewed billboard proliferation as essentially a political problem to which there must be a political solution. They believed that given enough time, enough expertise, and enough of Lawrence Rockefeller's money, a political solution through congressional action could be arranged.

Even Ed McMahon, who was open to differing views, initially saw billboards as simply pollution—not as a liturgical symbol representative of awesome and fundamental social, cultural, and psychic change. For Scenic America, its battle with the billboard industry was little different from any of the other attempts to control billboards over the previous fifty years. Tactics might by necessity change. Political allegiances might involve unexpected partners, such as minorities and antitobacco activists. Political and organizational realities might require hiring staff and professional lobbyists, where in the past volunteers would do. But fundamentally, billboards were simply a nuisance cluttering up an otherwise normal, unchanged, familiar landscape. Ironically and tragically, the real meaning and consequence of the great suburban transformation remained unknown to those who led Scenic America, at least until it was too late.

Scenic America failed to pass billboard reform legislation in Congress because it failed to see the social and cultural dimensions of the billboard issue. Political victory was dependent on being able to understand and respond to the reality of billboards in the same social and cultural venue in which they existed, the New American Landscape. Instead, Scenic America existed in self-imposed isolation. With only a few thousand members, support from a few historically prominent families and foundations, and employing a tiny staff, it attempted to achieve its objectives in the most public of forums—the Congress. Yet Scenic America deliberately and consciously did not seek out and form an alliance with the competitors of the billboard industry. Scenic America did not dissuade advertisers and advertising agencies from using billboards. It failed to pro-actively keep the issue of billboard control in the press and before the public. Scenic America took on the billboard industry in Congress, having deliberately isolated the conflict from those whose help was necessary to achieve passage of reform legislation.

The billboard lobby's political clout in Congress was matched by its business, social, and cultural clout outside the beltway. It cut special deals with the tobacco and liquor advertisers. It paid movie and television producers to include billboards in Hollywood films and television commercials (a subliminal method of gaining public acceptance). It donated free billboards to nonprofit and (surprise!) environmental organizations. The billboard industry was swimming in the mainstream of America's gaudy, commercially addictive cultural milieu. And where was Scenic America? Anywhere but in America, or so it seemed to me.

Influential officers of Scenic America feared any appeal from the organization to billboard advertisers to stop using billboards would result in instant lawsuits against Scenic America by the billboard industry, which would claim "restraint of trade." That truly successful nonprofit advocacy groups routinely endure harassing lawsuits did not appease their concern. Apparently they did not heed Chairman Mao's oft-repeated admonition, "if we are not attacked by the enemy, we have sunk to the level of the enemy."

The executive committee's adamant refusal to initiate rational and strategic action in its struggle with the billboard industry was a serious cultural inhibition. This became clear on the retirement of Ed McMahon, after long and exhausting years at the helm. The executive committee forcefully announced that McMahon's replacement would not come from the ranks of successful advocacy organizations like Hand Gun Control, Greenpeace, or the National Organization for

Women. Instead, McMahon's replacement came from the National Trust for Historic Preservation, an organization whose institutional conservative style the board of Scenic America related and aspired to.

Scenic America feared to recognize and admit even to itself that its agenda was to cause harm to a legal and lawful, albeit corrupt, industry—outdoor advertising. The majority of the executive committee had very effectively denied the obvious intention of Scenic America's legislative efforts (the harm or destruction of the billboard industry). The executive committee preferred to disguise those objectives in much more positive language, that of protecting the scenic and aesthetic qualities of the American landscape. Such subterfuge may have had its useful purpose. However, it was dangerous, for it blinded the organization to the ultimate implications of its actions. Too many on the inside did not accept what many on the outside instinctively understood Scenic America was all about. The more the organization succeeded, the more the billboard industry would lose money. Our friends and foes in Congress, our opponents in the industry, and knowledgeable members of the press certainly understood this. I grew increasingly certain that the executive committee did not, or would not.

For Scenic America's leadership, the nasty business of having to strategically confront the billboard industry was, to be frank, distasteful. The unarticulated but operative feeling was to let the politicians get their hands dirty while our board members stayed clean, above the fray. Most of all Scenic America was to remain aloof from such ungentlemanly tactics as cutting deals with whoever in the private sector might profit from outdoor advertising's misfortunes. In short, Scenic America's leadership wanted more to be perceived as cut from the same gentlemanly cloth as their counterparts at the National Trust than they wanted to do anything about billboards.

In the language of therapy, Scenic America was in a state of self-denial, denying the inevitable inverse proportion between the organization's success and the billboard industry's profitability. Such self-denial encompassed the inability to invoke a political solution to the billboard problem. Scenic America did not understand the necessity to deal with the billboard industry by employing the same familiarity and sense of ease with which the industry so capably subverted the public welfare.

Scenic America failed because it was burdened with the narrow and parochial views of highly successful but out-of-touch elitists. The elitists at Scenic America had no real understanding of the New Man and, worse yet, failed to grasp the vital necessity to acquire such understanding. Scenic America was not so much defeated by an aggressive billboard lobby as it was subsumed by a ubiquitous and powerful American culture it simply did not understand.

As the billboard lobby schemes to further commercialize all public space, a more proactive and culturally attuned Scenic America leadership may yet set a more assertive course. However, for the present Scenic America continues to pursue the aesthetic interests that seem so traditionally of intense concern to the leisured class: planting flowers along the highways, and trying to have what few unspoiled country roads that still remain, if not protected, than designated as something the organization likes to call "scenic byways." Such a whimsical, ethereal, ephemeral, and possibly meaningless designation has come to best characterize the one organization that once might have done something about billboards in America.

7 THE COMMERCIALIZATION
OF PUBLIC SPACE

In 1968 I was a senior philosophy major at Miami University in Oxford, Ohio. For four years I had taken only liberal arts courses, agreeing with my peers that the schools of business and education had little to offer the serious student. Nonetheless, I became determined not to graduate without having exposed myself to what I perceived to be the unworthy and Philistine curricula of one of those two lesser schools.

I enrolled in introductory advertising. On the first and every subsequent day the class met, the professor entered the room, reverently approached an unlighted glass display case, and solemnly illuminated a box of Tide laundry detergent, whose exhibit as a consumer icon served some exemplary purpose. It was not until the class had begun its discussion of outdoor advertising that I realized the extent to which the barbarians had indeed breached the very walls of academia. "Overcomes the boredom of traveling through the countryside," the professor of advertising declared to the class, as he touted the merits of billboard proliferation in America. Like the contemptible little intellectual lemmings they were, all the conservative business majors and no-brain jocks took exhaustive notes enumerating the many ways billboards enrich our lives.

Aghast, I turned from side to side, searching the faces of my classmates. I longed to find on just one face, any face at all, the same shock and dismay I felt at such a short-sighted and self-serving endorsement of a menace multiplying on the landscape. My search for one man or woman who had the aesthetic sensibility to find such effrontery unacceptable was for naught. Once again, I found myself the sole voice of rationality and sensitivity in a classroom full of barbarians.

"Yes, Mr. Miller," the professor yawned, barely holding back his weariness at having to deal with the protester from the school of liberal arts. "How have I offended you, this time," he asked.

With all the innate diplomacy of which even at that young age I was capable, and with a tone of voice so sweet, so agreeable, as to give no offense to the coarsest and most ill-bred of men, I proceeded to make known the case against the horror of billboards. Carefully, I did not base my objections on aesthetic grounds, for to do so in the school of business would have been to invite not only defeat but ridicule as well. No, I craftily objected to the ubiquitous billboard as a threat to the impression the advertiser really wanted to achieve, arguing that his product deserved a more acceptable and upscale advertising medium. My objections were not to be met with acceptance by either the professor or my classmates, for according to the consensus that readily emerged, I had failed to appreciate the key reason why billboards were fast becoming not only acceptable to advertisers but imperative.

"Because, Mr. Miller," the professor emphasized for my benefit, "thousands, hundreds of thousands of highway trav-

The Commercialization of Public Space

elers on our glorious interstates are bored to death staring at nothing but nature." He made his point without the slightest doubt or hesitation.

I stared incomprehensibly, unable to fathom the extent to which this man was certain our fellow Americans had so readily and completely abandoned their sense of aesthetics. How truly naive I was, even amid the drugs and illicit sex of the 1960s.

"Bored to death, Mr. Miller," the professor pressed on, oblivious to my incredulity. "Turned off to trees, corn fields, farmhouses, to the barren and unadorned earth," he added for good measure.

Silently, I listened and contemplated the man's meaning.

"Billboards," he went on, glancing upward, no doubt to some Platonic billboard in the ether, "will be no threat to the good advertisers who are wise and foresighted enough to use them." He intoned his words with growing confidence. "Yes, Mr. Miller, you will no doubt learn what many of us already know," he insisted, as if admonishing me for an unforgivable indiscretion. "Billboards will save the traveling public from being bored out of their minds."

"What minds?" I wondered aloud.

After twenty-five years my professor's remarks continue to speak volumes about the mentality and sensibilities of the average American. According to *Consumer Reports,* U.S. companies spent $125 billion on all advertising in 1991, compared to $12 billion for all advertising in 1960. Expenditures would not have been increased had advertising not been effective and well received by the public. The proliferation of outdoor advertising in the form of billboards—and, more perniciously, in the positioning, form, and style of buildings,

The Commercialization of Public Space

streets, and other components of the New American Land-scape—suggests two conclusions about Americans.

First, we can affirm that many people are simply oblivious to all forms of advertising that color, intrude on, and degrade the environment. One is tempted to presume that such an inability to notice commercial messages is indicative of their failure to attract attention. Nothing could be further from the truth. That part of the public that is oblivious to the com-mercialization of our environment is oblivious because ad-vertising messages are so very successful. The public's inabil-ity to see and to be conscious of billboards and other forms of advertising is a psychological defense mechanism. Such a defense enables individuals to retain and maintain some level of sanity in an environment that is increasingly designed visually and psychologically to accost them with commercial solicitations.

For many of our fellows, their blindness to the environ-ment and numbness to commercial appeals is the price they pay to survive. This raises several questions: Is such numb-ness reserved exclusively to filter out intruding commercial messages? Or, does it prevent consciousness of noncommer-cial phenomena as well? What is the broader social implica-tion of inadvertently and subconsciously encouraging people to become insensitive and oblivious to their environment as a means of coping and survival? Can and should uncon-sciousness be considered a social good?

Equally troubling is the view that a growing number, per-haps a majority, of the American public is very conscious of billboards and other commercial manipulations in our envi-ronment. The majority may find such solicitations entertain-ing, often richly rewarding, and not at all manipulative. This

The Commercialization of Public Space

is the theory that explains the acceptance of outdoor advertising as a source of instruction in the liturgy of self-definition through acts of consumption.

Few would deny that billboards are an indicator of just how blatantly commercial we have permitted the environment to become. It is no exaggeration to explain that the billboard industry is intent on the further commercialization of all public space. As I have pointed out, billboards are everywhere. They blight rural areas along interstates, downtown urban centers, industrial zones, and routes to tourist destinations. In some cities, billboards bring commercialism even to residential neighborhoods.

Billboards stand tall on the very borders of parks, across from schools, churches, hospitals, and even within sight of cemeteries. Billboards are commonplace on the sides of buses and on public bus stops. Some cities are permitting small billboards to be placed on parking meters. Who can forget that the U.S. Senate once seriously debated selling advertising space on mail trucks and neighborhood mailboxes?

Billboards have been erected on ski lifts in the Sierra Nevada and on kiosks at numerous golf courses. Little League fields in Santa Clara, California, no doubt trying to emulate the big leagues, now sport billboards advertising local merchants. Pacific Bell is permitting billboards to be erected on its public telephone booths. Soft drink vending machines, though officially on-premise signs and not billboards, formerly were adorned with small Coke or Pepsi logos. In the past few years, these soft drink machines have become six-foot vertical signs that just happen to dispense soft drinks.

Billboards are proliferating *inside* American buildings too. We have long been accustomed to billboards inside airport

The Commercialization of Public Space

terminals, on airport luggage carousels, and inside shopping malls. Billboards are now appearing in public rest rooms and on supermarket shopping carts. In Virginia, I have seen billboards in public junior high schools, advertising candy of course.

As this is written, plans are afoot to place commercial messages on the side of American spacecraft. According to the *San Francisco Examiner,* Space Marketing Inc. of Roswell, Georgia, hopes to launch the first "free standing" space billboard soon. "We could fly a corporate logo such as McDonald's Golden Arches into space and it might appear as large as the full moon," the company's president is reported to have said. The city of Atlanta considered the idea to help promote the 1996 Olympics.

In recent years the billboard industry has begun to contend openly that billboards constitute art and has promoted the notion that we should evaluate individual billboards for their effectiveness, artistry, and eye-catching appeal. Marshall McLuhan would have understood the billboard industry's need to seduce the public into focusing attention on the message and not the medium. He would correctly point out that, as with television, the power and pervasiveness of the billboard medium are not a function of the content of individual billboards. Their power is in the overall and cumulative impact of the collective medium. In a very real sense, we are not solicited by individual billboards; we are solicited by billboards as a phenomenon.

We can choose to react to and evaluate this increasing commercialization in a very literal way. We can argue that advertisers and billboard companies do not have a right to appropriate public space and to assault individuals with inescapable commercial messages, that they do not have the right to pass the cost of those messages on to the captive audience they accost. We can choose to deal with billboards simply as larger-than-life television commercials and ask the embarrassing question, where is the program? What are we, the audience, getting in return for being forced to "watch" outdoor commercials that play perpetually on our streets and highways?

On a more fundamental level we can ask what the implications are of such a dramatic change in our environment, caused in large part by the excesses of the billboard industry. Yes, we may all be spending more on products and services that perhaps we really do not need or even want. More indisputable is that the commercialization of public space has made the unimaginatively crass and unspeakably tasteless polite and acceptable.

One listens with some degree of amusement to those, especially among the religious right, who never tire of condemning what they consider the proliferation of sexual pornography. Far more pervasive and pornographic is the pornography of the hard sell that we have allowed to destroy the beauty, the sense of order, and, one can argue, the sanity, of our society. Billboards hawking booze and cigarettes nearby schools in many American cities are far more dangerous to the values of control, restraint, self-denial, and deferment of gratification than the availability of pornographic tapes in an adult video store.

Our daughters and mothers are not in real danger of being forced to watch people make love. Yet each day they are subjected to the most grotesque and vile commercial solicitations, the intrusiveness and inanity of which would have shocked our collective sensibilities only a few short years ago. Today we do not consume to live. We live to consume. According to a very popular biography in the 1920s, Jesus was a salesman. In the final decade of the twentieth century, we have demonstrated through the cumulative alteration of our physical landscape that when all is said and done, not just our God but our very lives are dedicated to sales.

The success of billboards as an advertising medium reminds one of television. One cannot exaggerate the effectiveness of television as a means of advertising. Television has succeeded both as an audience delivery system and, more fundamentally, as an agent of audience creation. Television, as the dominant form of communications and a cultural institution of immense influence, has appropriated many of the former sources of normative values. In their place, television has generated its own values, among them immediacy, impatience, and instant gratification, both emotional and intellectual. Television, the ultimate mechanism for forging autonomy and atomism while creating the illusion of community, forces the faithful viewer to focus fundamentally, not on the program content, but on him- or herself. Television is the ideal communications mode for a narcissistic age defined by therapeutic values.

In essence, television has succeeded because it has created a new environment that has displaced and eclipsed the real, nontelevison environment. One is so certain of this—intuitively, anecdotally, and statistically—that one is comfortable asserting that the essential test of a thing's reality is its acknowledgment by television. If something is on television, it is real. If it is not on television, it quite simply is not real.

There is an analogy between television and the New American Landscape. Outdoor advertising, like commercials in the television medium, is the obvious source of commercial solicitation in the new medium of our synthetic environment. Billboards, like television commercials, encourage the notion that advertising is entertaining, that advertising is art, that advertising is informative, that advertising may be newsworthy, and that advertising on a gigantic scale is permissible. In much the same way television commercials have debased the programming of television, as programs ape the successful artistry of television commercials, billboards have become the model for other components of our synthetic environment, as the designs of our retail and office buildings, streetscapes, and residential neighborhoods ape the obvious giganticism and overwhelmingly intrusive approach of the billboard. Retail, commercial, and even residential architecture is "in your face," if not down your throat. Individual consumers need to be psychologically reminded of the awesome power for individual definition inherent within the temples of consumption.

113

The values of commercials have gradually become the values of entertainment shows and even news programs. So too the form and style of overt commercialism is being adopted by those institutions that have traditionally existed and functioned outside the realm of the commercial: schools, homes, and institutional facilities of all types.

For some time we have been told that American education is in trouble, that academic standards at all levels have fallen. Johnny can't read, can't write, and will not be able to hold a job when he graduates. Worse yet, single parent families, child neglect and abuse, drugs, crime, the high cost of health insurance, and a host of other societal problems affecting

The Commercialization of Public Space

children are ending up in the laps of overworked, under-funded teachers. There are those who contend that the entire public school system is at risk of collapse, both in terms of continued financial support from hard-pressed local governments and from the growing dissatisfaction of disappointed and disapproving parents. The solution to all this, we are told, is to get serious: return to basics; raise teacher salaries and teacher performance; further involve parents in the classroom; and, in some cases, put metal detectors at the school-room door. To the metaphoric sensibility there is more here to be understood.

American schools, especially high schools, have seldom been certain of their true role. The debate about what constitutes a fit and proper public school education has been under way for well over 100 years. The curriculum has been shuffled accordingly—from classics, to sciences, to civics, to computer training and sex education. Through it all, American schools have been pursuing their real objective: to serve as the single institution that has the potential to involve children, parents, extended families, and the neighborhood at large in coming-of-age rituals that symbolically unite communities in a distinctly American fraternal bond.

Pedagogy is always a dead give away of what educators are really up to. The emphasis in the schools on technology and the hardware of television monitors, satellite dishes, and computers is a smoke screen for our education system's inability to engage, interest, and ultimately educate our students. The emphasis on gadgetry in American schools reveals their unarticulated but real decision to use television, movies, and computer games to compete with television, movies, and computer games for students' attention.

The Commercialization of Public Space

Metaphorically, our schools are not institutions of learning so much as nickel-and-dime imitators of the entertainment industry. Such a development should not come as an unpleasant turn of events to an elementary school teacher I know. She programs her VCR at home to tape daytime soap operas for evening viewing. With that kind of teaching mentality at loose in the American classroom, the Japanese must be squirming in glee.

If we were really serious about educational reform, we would open schools twelve months out of the year, require students to receive academic, not extracurricular instruction at least eight hours a day, and require at least half-day attendance on Saturday. We could pay for all of this by eliminating sports and other frivolous nonacademic activities. Rest assured, nothing remotely so radical as an alteration of our public school curriculum is likely to take place. If we were serious about reform, we would consider such drastic revisions to the status quo.

Whatever the content taught, the values inherent in a student's actual experience of the American education system today do not convey an appreciation for real scholarship—and they probably never have. Respect for ideas, intellectual accomplishment, self-denial, and a sense of deferment of gratification are not part of most school days. The real values of our public school system are the values of the broader society at large: sociability, amiable conformity, the ability to work as a team, and the life skills necessary to use a condom and balance a checkbook.

Education is now more than ever a product to be consumed. But as a product, education must compete with other products for the time and attention of student consumers.

The Commercialization of Public Space

The fate of education depends, not on an inherent and recognized claim on our adherence, but on its ability to compete successfully with other contenders for our time, attention, and loyalty.

Just as television has created a new environment that displaced and eclipsed the real, nontelevison environment, the New American Landscape is itself a new commercial environment that is in the process of displacing and eclipsing the real environment. Individuals and institutions on the New American Landscape will be increasingly defined by their ability to respond to, and function within, a commercial milieu in which everything, including ideas, will be advocated, understood, and accepted as products to be consumed.

The noncommercial environment of our immediate past is dead. In its place is the synthetic environment of the New American Landscape. Like any sophisticated communications channel, our new synthetic environment is capable of being connected to other dominant communication and information networks, such as television and the Internet. In fact, the New American Landscape is more than capable of being so connected; it is designed to be so connected.

The synthetic environment has the same inherent structural characteristics as does television; both are plastic, fluid, changeable, and immediate. These shared attributes permit a mutually enriching symbiotic relationship among television, the Internet, and the New American Landscape. Each feeds into and sustains the other. Each reinforces the other. Each reflects the mirrored image of the other. Each becomes the other.

At some primordial and fundamentally psychological level, the New Man will be unable to distinguish between the time

The Commercialization of Public Space

he is watching television, the time he is on-line, and the time he is physically moving through the environment. Each advertising medium will blend into the other, creating a perfectly seamless web, an all-encompassing modality of consumption—the quintessential twenty-first-century Utopia.

8 THE AMERICAN LANDSCAPE
THAT MIGHT HAVE BEEN

Though it was January, the bright sun and blue sky of a recent Sunday afternoon reminded me that in California, summer will not be confined to its own season. In California, summer insists on appropriating all seasons.

In California the hegemony of summer, even in the heart of January, seems only normal and to be expected. The New Man is very much at home in the protean reality of the New American Landscape. He has come to expect, in California at least, the environment and the weather to have the appeal and consistency of the figurative and literal atmosphere of a shopping mall.

In California the distinction between inside and outside has become as meaningless as distinctions among the designations urban, suburban, and rural—an observation I made in earlier chapters. Increasingly, for the New Man the only distinction worth noting regarding the environment is the degree to which it is designed to focus attention on the individual consumer. On the New American Landscape there are only two modalities. The first is focused on facilitating consumption, and the second is that which will soon be focused on facilitating consumption. Simply put, no other classification is possible. The implication is clear. The landscape is either actively facilitating individual and collective consumption or it has the potential to do so, to whatever varying degree.

The genesis and the realization of the New American Landscape need be understood not so much legalistically as culturally. The commercialization of public space and the facilitation of consumption are the purpose and character of the New American Landscape. This is not merely a function of the logical evolution of private property rights and free markets in operation. What we see in the New American Landscape is the culture of commercialism taken to an extreme though, in the minds of many, entirely and eminently logical conclusion.

The New American Landscape is much less a function of the inevitable operation of a consumer economy than the result of a deliberate choice on the part of all parties involved to embrace a total and comprehensive commercialism that knows no limits. The complete and total commercialization of public space is freely, if not enthusiastically, entered into by all societal groups, including consumers. In every sense that matters, the New American Landscape is very much the physical manifestation of a cultural consensus on the part of the majority of Americans. We are of course, talking about the culture of market values unmediated by any competing concerns.

I recall an experience in Bavaria. It was a moment in which I felt particularly receptive to the delightful interplay between the countryside and the tasteful, restrained Bavarian village. Inherently inoffensive in style, tone, and temperament, such places coexist peacefully with the natural envi-

The Landscape That Might Have Been

ronment. I was totally impressed with the harmony and balance I discovered there between the constructed environment and nature. I felt compelled to pay tribute to those wise and noble provincial lawmakers whose wisdom and foresight had mandated statutory safeguards ensuring the recognition, protection, and enhancement of the landscape's aesthetics.

"No," I was gently corrected. "There are no laws designed to protect the beauty of these villages," my host and guide informed me. No laws were necessary because no resident of a Bavarian village would, by custom, tradition, and sensibility, possess poor aesthetic judgment. Few would possess the simple bad taste to park a camper van in the driveway or exhibit a Virgin Mary birdbath or ceramic deer on the lawn. Such typically suburban grotesqueries are impossible to find in the civilized Bavarian countryside, let alone junked cars and towering billboards.

In Bavaria, apparently no laws are needed to protect the residents from themselves. Custom will suffice. However, custom is dependent on context. The New American Landscape exists outside of context, beyond history and nature, and beyond even a physical sense of place.

The New American Landscape is best understood when seen from behind the wheel of a car. The power of the car is not its ability to take us from one place to another. The power of the car is its context-defining windshield, which forces us to see our environment both intimately yet superficially, exactly as we see and understand the world when we watch television. Both the television screen and the car windshield create the illusion of intimacy and community while establishing and reinforcing the reality of autonomy and isolation.

The television experience is protean plasticity inside a box.

The Landscape That Might Have Been

As television creates us, we create it. As it bestows legitimacy on us, we in turn bestow legitimacy on it. With the advent of the New American Landscape, we are no longer boxed in by television. Plasticity is the essence of the new environment that powerfully replicates "outside" the raw, defining power of television's ability to reshape reality "inside." The transforming power of video is now unfettered and unbound.

As television destroys public life while anointing private life, the New American Landscape becomes the ultimate television screen on which we project our own private fantasies of the moment. The New American Landscape is a function of the perception of its inhabitants, and as their perception changes, is expected to change, and is encouraged to change, so too does the landscape. The social and physical reality of the New American Landscape, its very meaning and purpose, is dependent on the mediation of private individuals seldom able to think and act for purposes beyond themselves. The New American Landscape may be experienced by millions, but like television, it is experienced and infused with meaning privately and individually, not publicly and collectively.

Correspondingly, the New Man is most at home as an isolated, separate, disconnected individual—whether behind the wheel, before the television, or interacting with the computer. The networked virtual community of cyberspace called the Internet is hardly a community by virtue of its interactive nature so much as it is an illusion of community. Whether television, computer, or windshield, each screen is equally powerful at screening out any notion of the public realm while celebrating the essentially private and self-referential character of our new environment.

There can no longer be a public realm, peopled by public

The Landscape That Might Have Been

men, for the concepts to construct such realities no longer exist in an environment whose very essence is ad hoc. In this way the New American Landscape has escaped the limitation of time itself. We have all become time travelers able to move beyond the constraints of history as easily as we move on down the highway. The environment now speaks to us only in the present tense, enticing us to fulfill our immediate desires.

The chaos of the New American Landscape is ultimately a manifestation of the inner chaos that defines the New Man—rampant ego combined with blatant narcissistic self-indulgence. These characteristics do not create the compelling notion and resurgent theme that there is a whole man or whole society whose sum is greater than its individual parts.

Given the reality of the American landscape as a metaphor for the marketplace, it is difficult to imagine an alternative landscape—an American landscape that might have been. It is difficult, but not impossible. Instead of market forces defining the aesthetics of the American landscape, what if our landscape had been shaped by another institution or blend of institutions? What would be the look and feel of such an American landscape?

Imagine a landscape in which commercial activity was not visually and aesthetically dominant and the private passions of individuals were subservient to the public interest of the broader community. Imagine a landscape that was the product of the more traditional values of school, church, and family. How would such a landscape be different from the landscape we have come to inherit and occupy?

Any speculation about an aesthetically and ethically appealing alternative landscape is based on certain fundamental assumptions about its visual and aesthetic character:

— First and foremost, the landscape cannot exist visually and aesthetically as a mechanism for facilitating consumption and reinforcing notions of individual excess.
— By virtue of it being an alternative to private and individual concerns, an alternative landscape would be in spirit and purpose truly public. The majority of land visible to the public would legally remain in private ownership. However, the public landscape (regardless of whether privately or publicly owned) would not exist primarily to facilitate consumption or merely as "empty" space, awaiting development.
— An alternative and truly public landscape would be different from private and commercial space that was not visually and aesthetically part of the landscape. An alternative landscape would be space that in its appearance, in its dominant visual and aesthetic character, would emphasize public and communal values, even if its actual function were entirely and exclusively commercial. Such a dichotomy is not beyond current experience. One has only to consider a McDonald's fast-food restaurant housed in an authentic historic building, of which there are an increasing number.
— A landscape that emphasized public and communal values would not necessarily be inhospitable to the artistic, expressive, experimental, or even to that which was controversial. However, public space would be defined, above all, by noncommercial values, whatever they might be. Ulti-

The Landscape That Might Have Been

mately, the value of the public landscape would be precisely in proportion to its noncommercial appearance and visual character.

An alternative landscape would respect social and cultural issues in addition to environmental and aesthetic concerns. A truly public alternative landscape would tell a narrative—a story of who we were, who we are, and what we wish to become. By virtue of not being commercial, public space and the publicly visible landscape would be a manifestation not of private and individual excess but of communal and collective vision.

By being seen and perceived by all as a public asset, the public landscape would by necessity respect all, and in turn be respected. People do not litter and deface what they respect. This is the opposite of the New American Landscape that respects no one in its blind obedience to raw market values, and is little respected in return. By nature of this need to respect all, and its potential as a manifestation of shared vision, the public landscape would be by definition a product of deliberation, thoughtfulness, and judicious temperament. Such virtues sadly are lacking in our present landscape and society, which are so much a product of self-interest and self-indulgence.

By definition, a noncommercial public landscape would stand as a powerful force to literally alter our perception of time. A noncommercial landscape would not aid and abet the notion that all human activity and interaction need be defined by the commercial necessity to maximize efficiencies. In essence, a public landscape visually and aesthetically disassociated from commercial concerns would be a time machine, slowing down our increasingly accelerated, commercially defined lifestyle. The truly public landscape would be a corrective to the frantic intensity of market values.

Such desirable goals as appreciation for the environment, the arts, education, and disinterested contemplation would take on new viability by virtue of decommercializing the public landscape. Making the public landscape physically and visually manifest public concerns would be an immediate and powerful endorsement of noncommercial values and objectives by the society at large. There would be no more effective way to begin to change the public's attitude and behavior about itself and the environment than by decommercializing the landscape.

In essence, an alternative public landscape defined by some or all the characteristics I have described would encourage alternatives to the present hegemony of market values. Those alternatives, especially in terms of individual choices, might include numerous options. Most certainly one option would be an appreciation for, and endorsement of, what I have called traditional, nonmarket social values.

In a practical sense, the decommercialization of the American landscape would promote a new appreciation for past tradition. Decommercialization would also make possible yet-to-be-defined future alternatives to both traditionalism and the blatant self-indulgence of pervasive commercialism. The decommercialization of the public landscape is the most visible means of maximizing authentic individual and collective choice to accept to what extent commercial market values will define our lives. Such choices are meaningful alternatives to the tired old political clichés about big government and big business that express people's frustrations about the meaning of individual and collective identity.

Practically speaking, what do such abstractions mean? An alternative landscape would insure a minimum aesthetic standard for all highways, public works projects, and commercial development. An aesthetic standard would recognize the historic and natural character of particular geographic locations; it would mandate that commercial structures, especially retail outlets, conform to local aesthetic styles and reflect local historic values. An aesthetic standard would free highways from billboards and aesthetically hideous commercial signs. It would mandate outdoor works of art instead of outdoor advertisements. It would put electric, telephone, and cable television lines underground and out of sight.

Bountiful landscaping, environmentally compatible motorist directional signs, and graffiti and litter control would be the norm. Such legislation would inaugurate the serious planting of trees on the many millions of public acres adjacent to highways and streets. Certainly there are communities that have initiated some of these enhancements and controls, but they are few in number and influence.

Such aesthetic improvements and visual enhancements are only the beginning. Once we let go of the idea that private ownership and the functioning of free markets axiomatically necessitate the commercialization of all public space, many options become possible. An alternative public landscape would eventually assume numerous forms and landscape styles that would be sensitive to cultural and ethnic pluralism while establishing and maintaining meaningful aesthetic and environmental standards.

The Landscape That Might Have Been

The essence of an alternative public landscape assumes a relationship between a designated place and certain values that place represents. Such a landscape also postulates in its very existence the notion of an ongoing permanence that harkens back to an earlier epoch in history that would give meaning and continuity to future social innovation. Historically, temples and churches were designated sacred spaces. High mountains, the dismal swamp, and the dark woods were designated demonic spaces. Domestic space was of course manifest in the home and the notion that each man was to be accorded his castle, however humble. Public spaces were the commons and the square. Eventually, the state created, and the notion of public man sustained and nurtured, the public edifice. The public library, bridge, and park culminated in the beloved public infrastructure, so in danger today of withering away from inattention and underfunding. All of these distinct places, each with a distinctive identity, were the physical manifestation of particularly significant social values.

Societies composed of places with distinct identities offer individuals the opportunity to experience significant and different experiences of day-to-day living. In premodern, traditional societies, during a single day it is possible to move from the sacred to the profane and from the commercial to the domestic as one pursues one's personal affairs. Today's ego-driven narcissist has no need to acknowledge the sacred. Even his pretensions to spirituality are transparently therapeutic and profane. Few anthropologists would argue with the contention that in our secular, post-industrial society, sacred space does not exist, with the possible exception of the science lab and the therapist's office.

The Landscape That Might Have Been

In all but the most post-industrialized consumer economies, a distinct sense of place continues to define individual and collective behavior. Such identities of place present an alternative to modernity. Modernity is defined here by its ongoing and cumulative elimination of differences in physical place, which occur as it establishes one common experience of place. Additionally, modernity establishes ego, narcissism, and self-indulgence as dominant values. The most powerful example of the physical character and values of modernity is the New American Landscape, as I have defined it.

Of course, our alternative landscape is the physical manifestation of values that acknowledge and appreciate the desirability and even the necessity of a distinctive sense of place. As a naive and impressionable youngster in darkest Cleveland, at night I would often lie awake in my room imagining Los Angeles, a place I had never seen except in a thousand movies and television shows. Yet it was Los Angeles that for me stood as a shining alternative to the grim, blue-collar, industrial tedium of the steel mills and auto plants of my youth.

I was aware of New York, Washington, and even Paris and London as places that were obviously different from Cleveland and quite possibly able to liberate me from a prospective life at the Ford plant. Los Angeles, the city most representative of the very defining essence of modernity, was reshaping America.

As an impressionable ten-year-old, I understood that the Los Angeles experience was powerfully defined by southern California's mountains, deserts, and ocean—its unique sense of place. Paris and New York were provocative and intellectually stimulating. But it was diversity of place, and its promise

The Landscape That Might Have Been

of multiple options of personal behavior, that made the Los Angeles of my youthful fantasy so compelling.

Strange as it may seem to me now, as a ten-year-old Clevelander I imagined my life in Los Angeles as a series of passages. I would move progressively through the distinctly different but accessibly adjacent landscapes that made southern California so unique. My youthful fantasy always began with a morning hike in the Angeles National Forest. As the sun rose, I would search for the mountain lions that I knew lived there. I would attempt to make contact with the quintessentially untamed and primitive, whose ineffable essence so sharply contrasted with and enhanced the powerful forces of modernity at work in the valley below.

As the day progressed, I would descend from the mountain heights, my mood and behavior gradually changing. The visions and inspirations perceived by my inner eye in those rarefied realms burned less brightly with each descending step. My inner ear would pick up the chatter of the urban patois, and I would find myself becoming again inexorably connected to the rhythm of the city below. As the evening approached, and Apollo was subsumed by the seductive ministrations of Dionysus, I would spend a sophisticated night on the Sunset strip. Even as a ten-year-old, I would be able to negotiate the restaurants and night spots as deftly as, no doubt, I had transversed the hiking trails in the woods above.

In this boy's fantasy, my life in Los Angeles would be a life of experiencing on their own terms dramatically different places that in my child's mind existed in roughly the same geographical location. I was certain, even as a ten-year-old, that should I ever live in Los Angeles, I would lead a life impossible in New York, let alone Cleveland. I would not be just

The Landscape That Might Have Been

sampling variety and novelty like some kind of cultural consumer or cultural voyeur; I would experience the distinctiveness of places on their terms. Even then, I understood that anything less would be not so much to experience a place as it was to impose yourself upon it.

Over thirty-five years later, I am embarrassed by the irony that the reality of Los Angeles today is the opposite of my boyhood fantasy. No other place on the New American Landscape is better suited to the proclivities of the New Man. No other place has been so imposed on by private passions and individual greed—to the extent that it no longer has an identity free of pathology.

The failure of Los Angeles and its reshaping of American culture was not that it failed to nurture and sustain the natural environment surrounding the city. Almost every other metropolitan area has similarly failed to properly care for (or has destroyed) its immediate natural environment. The tragedy of Los Angeles, as the symbolic capital of modernity, lay in its power to bring about the death of public man and to substitute in his place private passions. This is the reality of substituting placelessness for a sense of place.

The New American Landscape is not so much a place as it is a nonplace. The values of its inhabitants, the new men, are not the values of place but of therapy, television, cyberspace, and other forms of placelessness. Desirable and humane values are, or have been, somehow connected to physical place, and the differences among and within places enrich our values and our lives.

Our alternative landscape, though hardly capable of achieving actual physical existence, does exist metaphorically in video space. The continuing popularity of old televi-

The Landscape That Might Have Been

sion shows like *Father Knows Best, The Donna Reed Show, Leave It to Beaver,* and *The Waltons* appeal to we who are placeless. This is precisely because such programs exude a palpable sense of place.

Of course, it is ironic that we must turn to the placeless medium of television to begin to appease our appetite for place. However, one can convincingly argue that we watch and love these shows because they offer us the best of television's places. I am not talking about simple nostalgia for the past. The television audience can sense the distinctiveness and desirability of Donna Reed's neighborhood without desiring to act out Donna's pre-feminist domesticity.

The continuing popularity of *Star Trek: The Next Generation* is also an example of our hunger for context through a sense of place. The *Enterprise,* now to be seen anew on the movie rather than the television screen, is more than a starship: it is the twenty-fourth century neighborhood of *Father Knows Best.* Jean Luc Picard is as much a father to his family in space as was Robert Young to his on the ground. In hostile space, the *Enterprise* is a ship not of war but of family values, which serves to distinguish its meaning from that of other places in the galaxy.

What one is likely to find in these neighborhoods is the opportunity to imagine something more, something better. It is not more money and more things but more meaning in a life that unfolds in, and not out of, context. These programs appeal to us because they occupy a place in which the seductive temptations of the market—its power to destroy place— are tempered and restricted.

In the 1950s sitcom neighborhood, the landscape restrains the marketplace. It buffers the market's potent aggressive na-

The Landscape That Might Have Been

ture with equally powerful countervailing physical spaces such as the church, the school, the public square, and the home. All of these distinct places expect individuals to behave appropriately, to change behavior to accommodate the physical space they occupy.

In television shows and in real societies in which places are different, a sense of place guides and informs individual behavior. When places have permanent identities and we adjust our behavior to accommodate those identities, individual behavior is a function, not only of personal pleasure and preference, but of social and cultural expectation. Sense of place thus becomes a conservative social force promoting tradition and historical continuity.

The behavioral expectations of place, far from being restrictive to individual behavior, actually enrich individual behavior. When identity and behavior are a function of place, and places are different from one another, ironically, a range of individual behavior is possible and expected. Choice and possibility are affirmed. Where physical place is a prime determiner of behavior, the often revered but seldom realized cultural pluralism, so important to us now, is real and not illusory. The Beaver's neighborhood provides the psychic space to be nurtured by both the restrictive and liberating aspects of a culture, not just the opportunity to succeed or fail in an economy. A culture rooted in a sense of place is a culture existing within history. A culture composed entirely of economic imperatives has neither a sense of place nor a place in history.

Our alternative to the New American Landscape bears a surprising structural similarity to almost any landscape of an earlier historical epoch. Even urban, commercial, and indus-

The Landscape That Might Have Been

trial landscapes of the late nineteenth century, possessing no beauty, tranquillity, human scale, or even hint of civility, inherently suggest to us all of these positive qualities and more. Such a landscape, even though grim and forbidding, offers to us a distinctive sense of place, and it is the distinctiveness of that sense of place that embodies within itself its own diametric opposite.

Yesterday, for each appalling dark satanic mill there was the implication of mill-less-ness. There existed an uncorrupted and untainted alternative in which the potential for a different and more welcome behavior was possible and to be expected. Mill-less-ness was a reality because obviously the entire environment consisted of more than the forces of industrial production. Today, as we witness the image of a dark satanic mall, there is no implication of mall-less-ness. There is no inherent postulating of an imaginable opposite to what has become the dominant configuration defining the New American Landscape.

When history mattered, youngsters could imagine leaving home for some place that was different. It could be the big city or the truly pastoral. Today, youngsters may dream about leaving home, but it is much more difficult to imagine a landscape of one's own personal future unlike the malled reality that has become so ubiquitous.

The emergence of the New American Landscape, while the result of specific historical and other forces so noted and defined, was not inevitable. Neither is the New American Landscape the unalterable product of time and history marching lockstep into an undeniable future not to our liking. At the risk of being accused as naive and optimistic, I believe the case can be made that the American landscape might well

The Landscape That Might Have Been

have escaped its apparent fate as the environmental manifestation of market values. One can argue convincingly that the landscape might have been spared appropriation by the worst forms of commercialism even as we maintained our faith in free markets and private property.

An alternative to the New American Landscape is not a socialist Utopia, as some might contend. There is nothing inherent in the free market system that requires the appropriation, negation, and reconstruction of the physical environment into a mechanism to facilitate aggregate consumption. However, the existence of our alternative landscape as a cognitive possibility seems increasingly implausible. The notion of limits and of clearly defined certainties have given way to a much more fluid, flexible, and perpetually changing view of physical and nonphysical reality. Such a view may owe its genesis in part to market values. However, the consequent effects impact the market and beyond.

The notion that cities and towns are defined includes the idea that they occupy particular physical space. The countryside lies outside those urban spaces. These divisions reflect a way of thinking that is particularly pre-modern. The New Man, driven by ego and the need for instant self-gratification, cannot be satisfied in a society defined, and physically designed, to reflect classical notions of pre-modernity.

As meaningful definitions of community and the public welfare become eclipsed by ego and narcissistic passions, the landscape, and all of public space, will no longer be a neutral zone of mutual and reciprocal respect for the rights, sensibilities, and privacy of others. The landscape cannot be the physical manifestation of an agreed-on and accepted neutral

The Landscape That Might Have Been

public sphere, off limits to the self-interest of any single particular group or individual.

Instead, in the New American Landscape, public space is transformed from a nonexploitative common ground into a hunting ground of commercial predation. The aesthetic dimension of the landscape exists to be exploited. In catering to our individual and collective narcissistic desires, the landscape becomes, not a haven from commercialism and utility, but merely another mechanism to facilitate commercialism and utility.

The Landscape That Might Have Been

9 THE INNATE PHILISTINISM OF THE ENVIRONMENTAL MOVEMENT

B y now, we are somewhat weary of the oft-repeated paraphrase of John Muir, founder of the Sierra Club, that any fool can cut down a tree, but it takes a wise man to preserve a forest. One is tempted to suggest that any fool can preserve a forest, but it takes a truly wise man to beautify and make livable the typical American community.

For those who are concerned about the aesthetics of the American landscape, the indifference and, at times, the hostility of environmentalists to aesthetic issues is profoundly troubling and disappointing. Over the years, those who have turned to the environmental movement for help in preserving and enhancing the aesthetics of the American landscape have been brushed aside. Often we have been labeled as kooks and loonies, much as environmentalists themselves were labeled in the bad old days, before we all fell in love with tropical rain forests and cuddly fur-bearing mammals.

To increase their legitimacy in the wake of growing public interest, mainstream environmentalists found it necessary to distance themselves from fringe groups and what the mainstreamers perceived to be fringe issues. Among the first to be abandoned by the Sierra Club and dismissed as no more than

little old ladies in tennis shoes were the fledging and unbelievably naive proponents of billboard control. Many could
trace their lineage to such Victorianesque organizations as
the Garden Clubs of America. Quaint and ineffectual, perhaps. Kooks and loonies, no.

The issue of billboard proliferation acquired a stigma
among mainstream environmentalists that it still cannot
shake to this day (no matter how visually polluted with
commercial messages our environment becomes). The environmental movement's refusal to recognize the legitimacy of
aesthetics is a function of the movement's insecurity and
longing for acceptance. Real and imagined environmental opponents argue that environmental regulations are an economic disincentive, framing the debate in nonaesthetic
terms.

As I have noted, early efforts to preserve Yellowstone and
Yosemite were centered on appeals to save scenery. Saving
ecosystems was an unknown idea. Yet today, appeals to
protect scenic beauty are for many environmentalists embar-
rassingly esoteric. In their rush to gain the widest possible
acceptance by the American public, the environmental community has decided that appeals to aesthetics are unscientific.
Mainstream environmentalists are much more comfortable
engaging their opponents with quantifiable, scientifically
validated arguments advancing scientific and economic reasons to protect the environment.

Environmentalists also feel that aesthetics smacks of a palpable patrician elitism that just will not appeal to the average
citizen. One suspects a certain calculation by environmentalists as they refused to seriously support the Highway Beautification Act and subsequent efforts at billboard control. Even

appeals for support by Lady Bird Johnson and old-money types such as Lawrence Rockefeller fell on deaf ears. Be it the very savvy and professional lobbyists of the Sierra Club or the street-fighting activists of Greenpeace and Earth First, no one in the environmental movement had time for aesthetics. Aesthetics was considered an illegitimate issue of interest only to the idle rich.

Before we rush to congratulate mainstream environmentalists for their egalitarian fervor, consider their need to discredit aesthetics as a fundamental weakness, a need that hints at the long-alleged but seldom identified dark side of organized environmentalism. Critics contend that environmentalists are antihistorical, antirational, and even antihuman. Such arguments are usually superficial and self-serving. Nevertheless, there may be some truth to these allegations.

Environmentalists are inclined to endorse and validate what they perceive to be natural, while accepting the manmade environment as a necessary evil. For many environmentalists, pristine wilderness is more than simply pristine wilderness. It is the source of all that is good, beautiful, truthful and inspiring. In stark and obvious contrast, the realm of the man made is, by definition, at best value neutral. At worst it is an irredeemable mechanism for the destruction of the natural world. Thus, the environmental mentality is predisposed to dismiss the man made, to consider the realm of the constructed environment and the collected works of man indivisibly and indistinguishably flawed. Such thinking quite obviously fails to acknowledge the difference between appropriate and inappropriate development, let alone recognize the

The Environmental Movement

aesthetic value inherent, or even potentially inherent, in the historic activities of man.

Environmentalists justifiably criticize those who fail to understand that man is part of the biological world and dependent on the biological world for survival and well-being. Yet environmentalists fail to understand that man is a function of his inherent need to exist as something more than one species among many. Man's self-identity is as an agent in history whose collective endeavors indelibly affect the life of our planet.

The problem for environmentalists, and for the rest of us, is how to accommodate our role as historical agents effecting change without destroying the planet in the process. The simple fact is that we cannot reverse history, erase our experiences and memory of the industrial revolution, and return to an allegedly more environmentally benign, agriculturally based world economy. Such suggestions are at best the product of starry-eyed utopian visionaries who have no knowledge of either history or human behavior. We cannot turn back the clock to a mythical Eden that never existed, if for no other reason than because too many people in the Third World covet microwave ovens and color televisions.

Rather than reverse history, we have no choice but to embrace history and deal with the present environmental crisis while remaining conscious of our role as historic agents effecting change. As the most enlightened of the environmentalists realize, the environmental crisis is really a crisis of our collective identity. Do we remain as we have been, profligate producers and consumers with little regard for those biological and other fundamental relationships and associations that sustain us and our entire planet? Or, do we redirect and rechannel our energies and our inquisitive, acquisitive, superrationality? Do we redirect those energies into ways of doing and thinking and being that will permit us to be ourselves without disrupting the biological equilibrium of the planet?

The environmental question increasingly becomes one of man's future identity and responsibility. That being the case, discussions of the environment, especially among thoughtful opinion leaders, need to be formulated psychologically, sociologically, philosophically, and perhaps even theologically. Unfortunately, and much to their longterm strategic misfortune, mainstream environmentalists have become enamored of arcane scientific disciplines. They mistakenly appropriate the language and values of physical science to impress the public with the urgency of the environmental case. We find that environmental discussion focuses on the particulars of ozone depletion, gill net fishing, and toxic waste disposal. One reluctantly accepts that what we have heard thus far from environmentalists—global warming, nuclear waste, dead whales, and other litanies of ecological destruction—is what we are destined to get, ad infinitum.

The public will not long respond to greater fear of ecological peril in the face of planetary business as usual. We have only a limited capacity to react to extremely negative assessments of our future welfare. Dire warnings of ecological doom will not infuse the residents of Egotopia with a sense of commitment but only a sense of despair. It is obvious that we have reached a saturation point concerning ecological catastrophe.

The public imagination will not be engaged by pleas to reinstate the Earth's self-regulating ecological mechanisms.

The Environmental Movement

Such appeals to optimum thermostatic functioning will elicit the enthusiasm they deserve. The complexity of the global environmental crisis, made increasingly complex by environmentalists themselves, will overwhelm our ever decreasing attention spans. Environmentalists are to be credited with putting environmental issues on the global agenda. But one senses that the environmental mainstream has no strategy to guide future public debate. Such debate seems perpetually destined to miss the essential point of defining how we choose to live in the next century and beyond.

The environmental agenda will not be realized if environmentalists, like military strategists captivated by the lessons of the last war, busy themselves battling an enemy that is no longer relevant. Capitalism; greed; corporate excess; amoral, immoral types on Madison Avenue and in the White House poisoning the planet for profit—these are the old villains, the bad, old images that environmentalists, armed with scientific data and speaking technical jargon, employ to convert and enlist the American public.

Of course, the fundamental realities with which we must all contend are those of education as entertainment, of work as an opportunity for self-expression, of the self-absorbed narcissist seeking sustenance and meaning from therapeutic values. These are the images shaping both the forces of production and the forces of consumption, defining both the powerful and those who covet power, both the perpetrator and the victim. In every quarter, the New Man is on the move and the old communal values in jeopardy, not from the bad old images but from the new realities that define our present dark age.

It is incumbent on environmentalists, as drivers and definers of the ecological debate, to understand the coming of the New Man. The New American Landscape offers a palpable focal point of resistance to those who sense the inability of therapeutic values to provide and sustain individual and social meaning. The old environmental bogeymen of greed, corporate excess, and bad guys in the White House need to be replaced by their contemporary counterpart: the New Man, hungry for meaning in an increasingly meaningless New American Landscape.

Environmentalists should direct their rhetoric toward, not bashing the New Man, but saving him from the common enemy—himself. Such a reordering of the environmental perspective will depend on a more comprehensive understanding of history and human behavior than the environmental movement has so far demonstrated. Environmentalists need to realize that history is a record of our past actions and as such implies that we will be equally active in the future. Human history does not coexist with nature but impacts nature. The choice we make lies in the way we do so.

A sense of posterity invites us to postulate an environmental vision of our collective future, a vision that takes us beyond the narcissism, the self-absorption, the materialism, and the decadence of our present age. Surely the continued and growing popularity of science fiction on television is due to more than the public's fascination with technology. Such popularity is a function of a pent-up, unrealized, inarticulate aspiration that the future will have meaning beyond the meaninglessness of the present. Oh, to be one of the crew of the starship *Enterprise,* to belong to something greater than ourselves. Why is it a mere television program has offered to so many what family, religion, and therapy apparently have

The Environmental Movement

not? The public imagination, such as it is, must be addressed, solicited, and enticed by a vision. That vision should be of an environmental future that is an alternative, not to the excesses of our industrial past, but to the excesses of our narcissistic present.

Environmentalists have no vision of the future to offer the public because environmentalists have no imagination to engender such a vision. The best environmentalists can propose is pristine wilderness without the contaminating presence of man. Of course, the challenge is not only to preserve wilderness but to create a livable, aesthetically enriched, man-made environment that degrades neither the natural environment nor itself.

143

A future environmental vision must amount to more than planetary ecosystems functioning normally. Only an authentic and genuine vision will excite the imagination and engage the support of a restless public searching for something meaningful in which to believe. Such a vision acknowledges that environmentalism must begin at home, within the environment in which 98 percent of us spend 98 percent of our time. A future environmental vision needs to emphatically demonstrate that the man-made environment will be different and better in a world honoring ecological values.

How beauty will play a decisive role within the man-made environment of an ecologically sensitive future is the key to enticing, exciting, and engaging what remains of our collective imagination. The revolution will not be one of guns, self-renunciation, and the smashing of our technological golden goose. Rather, the revolution will be an evoking of our long-repressed aesthetic awareness that, in Jungian terminology, is a collective human archetype awaiting to emerge at our clarion call.

Make no mistake. Appeals to beauty cannot be pale, anemic intellectual exercises. Abstractions will not faze the thick-skinned and dull-witted New Man. His cognitive capacities have been anesthetized by both media and the manipulative, debilitating environment we now call home. Denied his intellect, uninformed of his history, uneducated in the ways of the broader world, immune to the persuasiveness of reason, the New Man is capable only of understanding and of acting emotionally.

Like the savage beast of the fable, he awaits the soothing ministrations of the aesthetic muse. Fortunately, the essence of the aesthetic experience is pure emotion—on tap, in reserve, powering the principal modalities of our post-industrial consumer society. Even financially strapped, budget-busted environmentalists may use emotion in passionate aesthetic celebrations to influence and motivate the hungering masses.

If only environmentalists could sense that aesthetics is the missing link capable of tying together the increasingly loose ends of the environmental agenda. Desperately, we need a unifying force that compels the public to commit to a defining and renewing environmental future, a future that is more than the equivalent of an engineering pledge to keep the planet's plumbing systems in optimal operation. As environmentalism deteriorates into deliberations of eco-engineering technique, aesthetics offers the opportunity for transcendence beyond the stultifying sterility, narcissistic indulgence, and therapeutic excess of the New American Landscape.

The Environmental Movement

An increasingly enlightened federal government may begin to assume its long-ignored environmental responsibilities by initiating proper management of our ecological systems. The mainstream environmental organizations will need to do what they have always needed to do, stay ahead of public agencies in defining the critical environmental issues of the day. Unfortunately, I see no evidence to suggest that the environmental community understands its opportunity to play the aesthetic card in redefining the language and the meaning of the environmental debate. Tactically and strategically, now is the time to make aesthetics the unifying theme of the environmental agenda.

Environmentalists must integrate their love of the natural with a renewed understanding and appreciation of the man-made environment. Ultimately, we can have neither pristine wilderness nor aesthetically fulfilling communities without a new way of thinking about the total environment. Long ignored and repressed, the fundamental aesthetic sense common to all mankind offers us a means to bridge the conceptual and emotional gap between the natural and the man made. We await a model for creating and re-creating the landscape as a synthesis of man and nature.

No longer can environmentalists fight to protect such places as Great Smoky Mountains National Park and then turn their backs on society's encirclement of these preserves with choking collars of commercial development. As a man never at a loss for words, Marshall McLuhan wisely informed us years ago, "the whole world's a national park." It is time the environmentalists caught on.

The Environmental Movement

10 DEMOCRACY, THERAPY, AND
THE TRIUMPH OF BAD TASTE

One cannot examine the causes of our wretched aesthetic condition without acknowledging a certain historic inevitability to our present circumstances. What charm, what beauty, what grace we once enjoyed in those oh-so-distant days of our nation's innocent youth. Such qualities have been sacrificed in return for the physical and financial means to create, nurture, and sustain history's largest and most inclusive middle class.

America is the world's golden goose, perpetually laying golden eggs. America calls to both the world's entrepreneurs and the huddled masses, each yearning, in the axiom of the Vulcan sage, "to live long and prosper."

The historical perspective often permits and encourages such a generous and accepting view. However, in the sharp and unforgiving light of morning, as one confronts the grim and foreboding reality of the New American Landscape, the need for further explanation is palpable and raises several questions: Why have we permitted the most base elements of our society to determine how America looks and feels? Why have we permitted our public spaces to become foul and mean? We are a society that prides itself on our apparent ability to "have it all," to create "win/win outcomes," to "empower" our fellows so they may vanquish even the most debilitating depression. Why cannot such a society enjoy economic prosperity without suffering its own aesthetic destruction? The answers to such questions suggest a heuristic relationship among our commitment to political democracy, our love of money, and our increasing acceptance of therapeutic values. Let us begin with our genuine and admirable democratic convictions.

Democracy is a process as much as it is an end. As a process, the democratic disposition has not remained idly at rest. Since the beginning of our republic, we have relentlessly struck down elitist barriers designed to impede participation of the common man in affairs of state. In the early years, not only were blacks and women denied the vote, but those without property and the correct religious affiliation were consigned to the political outside looking in. The democratic impetus to bestow citizenship on the disenfranchised and to elicit expanded participation in the political process demonstrates that our definition of democracy is not static and constant but organic and evolving.

It was not long before those who had won the vote were able to use their political power to further their economic interests. Agitation by organized labor, progressives, populists, and socialists in both the nineteenth and twentieth centuries put economic concerns squarely on the political agenda. By the twentieth century, increasing numbers of people were able to vote.

As the depression made its horrendous impact felt, the democratic notion that all citizens, by virtue of their citizenship, were entitled to a basic level of economic security be-

The Triumph of Bad Taste

came a legitimate political issue. Years earlier, Henry Ford was one of the first American industrialists to understand that the common man needed higher wages, not just to survive but to be able to buy automobiles and other big-ticket items that, by the dictates of economies of scale, needed to be mass produced.

Mass consumption by an American public enjoying ever increasing real earning power had become much more than an issue of economic security. Higher wages were an absolute necessity for the success of twentieth-century industry. Ultimately, both political parties accepted the view that the federal government needed to play a serious role in combating economic depression and guaranteeing an ever expanding economy. Since the dawn of the postwar era, a mighty political consensus has worked diligently to foster and promote ever increasing purchasing power by the common man. In effect, we made a political commitment to expanding the size and influence of the middle class. One could argue that, in order to reassure the entire electorate, both political parties agreed on certain basic principles: full production, full employment, and full consumption. Disagreements were not, as was so fondly said, over ends but over the means to achieve those ends.

The beginnings of the great suburban transformation reflected a political and economic consensus that brought to the middle decades of this century a certain stability and prosperity. We, in our era of too rapid change and threatening uncertainty, now romanticize this period. The obvious political influence of the common man was making itself felt in political resolutions of fundamental questions of economic

The Triumph of Bad Taste

security. This should not be surprising. Provide the common man with a public primary and secondary education. Make easier his access to higher education. Guarantee his right to vote and participate in the political process. Assure his equal standing within the judicial system. Meaningfully increase his wages (with notable lapses in the case of minorities and women duly noted). Do these things and the very essence of capitalism becomes modified, as political democracy breeds some degree of economic democracy.

There is a cynical opinion, especially among liberal intellectuals, that democracy is perhaps more an illusion than a reality. Such criticism suggests that we enjoy precious little political democracy, as evidenced by what they note is an ever increasing economic inequality. Such a view suggests a reoccurring imposition on the people by a ruling oligarchy that has co-opted both political parties. I would refute that view. This exposition has demonstrated that democracy is not just a means of making political choices. Nor is it only a means of asserting one's economic interests. Democracy's vital influence is particularly evident in how the political and economic interests of the common man are manifest as cultural icons within the broader society at large.

Edward Bellamy, now long-forgotten, was a utopian socialist in the late nineteenth century whose novel *Looking Backwards* even today makes for amusing reading. Often he forced his characters to stop in mid-plot and ask the ideological question, when would the common man take his economic destiny into his own hands? (It was the kind of question socialist writers in those earlier days liked to ask their readers with great regularity.) As I have attempted to demonstrate, the common man has certainly taken his aesthetic destiny, and ours as well, into his own hands and will, I fear, never let go.

In matters of taste, style, and form of expression, the aesthetic history of much of the twentieth century is the history of the rebellion of the common man. He has rebelled against those who would impose from above some elite standard of aesthetic excellence. Such a cultural revolt would not have been possible, or likely, had not the democratic impetus succeeded both politically and economically. Democracy succeeded, not just through including the common man in the broader economic and political culture, but, more fundamentally, through permitting the common man to re-create the broader culture in his own image.

Surely this is as significant an expression of democracy as is electing a president. Could the liberal intellectuals have forgotten that Ronald Reagan and a great number of conservative Republicans are not the sons and daughters of the landed gentry? Hardly a hereditary ruling class, they are very much the heirs of humble and common origins. In that regard, are they not mythically entitled to high public office?

One can certainly make the case that our democracy has never been more robust. The democratic impulse that for over 200 years has succeeded in expanding political power and opening economic issues to political resolution has largely, although with notable exceptions, succeeded in fulfilling those objectives. (If we are not a socialist state, it is not because we are undemocratic. It is because a majority repeatedly rejects socialism in favor of the status quo.)

Our great democratic passion has for some recent indiscernible period asserted its most prodigious energies not po-

150

litically and economically but culturally. Not only politically and economically are we increasingly defined by the interests, values, and aspirations of the common man. Ours is very much a society in which cultural and aesthetic choices are decided democratically, not in the voting booth but at the shopping mall.

Just as political parties in a democracy by definition appeal to the common man, without whose votes they would not be elected, economic interests providing consumer goods and services must also appeal to the common man. Such appeals are far more productive when the cultural icons of a post-industrial consumer society are in tune with the culturally dominant majority.

It is instructive to point out that the New American Landscape we have been describing is not the America of old money. It is not even the America of new money. We are today the America of mass money. Mass money is the disposable income of the great, unwashed public, yearning and aspiring openly and unashamedly to create itself anew through redemptive acts of frenzied consumption.

As we have seen, the powers inherent in the formation, expansion, nurturing, and ultimate supremacy of the great suburban transformation have had their roots in the common soil. They have flowered in the face of withering, and often justifiable, criticism from pundits of the right, left, and center. The suburban transformation has produced both men and values that appear immune to the criticisms of the traditional elites. In the closing years of this tired century, the common man has driven those defeated elites into a permanent cultural exile.

The very rich, the very intellectual, and the very radical (if such radical elements do in fact exist as other than comic relief) are simply no longer relevant to those who comprise the great suburban transformation. The battle between Scenic America and the billboard industry was a little-noticed morality play in which the old order failed not only to defeat but to comprehend the new.

The aspiring middle class was born to greater achievements in the postdepression, postwar, postindustrial economy that has characterized much of this century. It has cast off the political, moral, intellectual, and aesthetic leadership of America's traditional elites and forged, not only a new suburban home, but a new suburban standard by which to measure and be measured.

In place of rigid hierarchies of evaluation, our New Man seeks the solace and protection of an all-forgiving therapeutic dispensation. He does his thing. He centers and grounds himself. He gets in touch with his feelings. He acknowledges his hurting and misunderstood inner child. He attempts to recall his repressed memories of a dysfunctional childhood. Above all else, he expresses and re-expresses himself to friend and acquaintance alike. The new standard of behavior is not how well we treat others but how well we indulge ourselves.

We have seen political democracy evolve into economic democracy and further still into cultural democracy. At some undefined but real point, under the unrelenting pressure of rising expectations, the democratic impetus mutated. It transformed into a curious egalitarianism. This suggests that our cultural modalities are not a function of demonstrated authority and wisdom but of asserted desire. Our cultural icons and myths are no longer the function of collective memory,

The Triumph of Bad Taste

tradition, experience, or education but of the raw and emotive assertion of our naked and shameless selves.

T. S. Eliot delivered a lecture in 1939 at Christ College, Cambridge. The noted poet contended that "the tendency of unlimited industrialism is to create men and women of all classes, detached from tradition, alienated from religion, and susceptible to mass suggestion: in other words, a mob. And a mob will be no less a mob if it is well-fed, well-clothed, well-housed and well-disciplined." What might Eliot say were he alive today and a-wandering on the New American Landscape?

Such explanations of our current wretched aesthetic condition are not particularly original. One is reminded of José Ortega y Gasset's *Revolt of the Masses,* the English translation of which first appeared in 1932. Ortega y Gasset, the noted Spanish political philosopher, warned that the common man was on the move. The common man was about to take control of the political and cultural levers of power, about to assert himself in such previously elitist turf as literature and the arts.

And so we return again to the essential question with which we have been struggling throughout the pages of this volume. Why have we permitted the most base elements of our society to determine how America looks and feels? Why have we permitted our public spaces to become foul and mean? There are many meaningful answers, but, of them all, perhaps the most informative is also the most curious.

Let us accept T. S. Eliot's view that we have, through our industry and technology, created and institutionalized a mob. We have permitted that mob to set for us our societal

153

standards, cultural icons, and norms of behavior. Accepting this as so explains briefly why we have permitted the most base elements of our society to determine how America looks and feels. We simply have been guilty of unthinking generosity.

In a very basic and fundamental way the American attitude and experience were born of generosity. We enjoyed abundant, almost infinite natural resources. Pragmatically, we recognized and rewarded initiative and performance above birth and inherited wealth. We benefited from that most revolutionary and least understood attribute of capitalism, its openness to all with capital, regardless of position, religious, or political affiliation (exceptions for women and minorities duly noted).

From the earliest days we were a generous people. Our sense of generosity has been flawed by an inability to understand that our generosity, successively unrestrained by broader communal values, would mutate into greed, license, and self-absorption. In our generosity sprouted the seeds of imbalance, disharmony, and hubris, afflictions that sapped the moral fortitude of our aspiring middle class. Those among us who might have known better fell captive to a spirit of egalitarianism. It tempted us to believe that all people are morally equal and equally capable of determining standards to instruct their behavior.

Our growing faith in the redemptive power of our technology seduced us into believing that the generosity of our spirit could be matched by a generosity of resource and capability. In the technologically exciting decades that have brought us personal computers and condoms that glow in the dark, we have become convinced that given enough time, enough

The Triumph of Bad Taste

money, and enough expertise, all things, both material and immaterial, are possible.

Having been so generous in these decidedly American views of our collective potentiality as to shrink from the exercise of moral and normative authority, we have arrived at that point in history when it is time to say no to those who would continue to consume and debase our common aesthetic heritage. So long have we been devouring our moral capital that even those satiated on the heady narcissistic nutrients that flow so generously from our cultural troughs may realize that their gluttony foretells a mighty fall.

155

11 BREAKING THE SPELL
The Future of the New American Landscape

s I prepared to begin writing this final chapter, across an overpass of a freeway near my home hung a banner proclaiming, "We Are in the End Time—Get Right with Christ." The fundamentalist Christians, with their dire warnings about an end time, have appropriately set the stage for the apocalypse. Instead of Christ's arrival to rapture his followers away to Heaven, we must confront the Antichrist, not of the fundamentalist Christians, but the real Antichrist: our own worst selves turned loose and unrestrained on the physical and moral landscape.

The aesthetic degeneration I have carefully chronicled in these pages speaks not just to the outward ugliness of our vast consumer society. It demonstrates Egotopia's inner ugliness— a debilitating defect of collective character that has the capacity to ultimately destroy the last vestiges of civility. The billboards, the blight, the daily circus we call television, the frantic madness down at the local mall we call shopping— these manifestations of contemporary society all have meaning. They symbolize our collective obsession with ourselves, portending the end of one world and the beginning of the next.

One cannot contemplate the New American Landscape and fail to believe that the old order is quickly passing into history. Traditional society has been paved over by the New American Landscape. That is the bad news. The good news is that one cannot chronicle the ascension of the self, the false redemptive grace of therapeutic values, the establishment of mass sensibility in all things, and the hollowness of rampant materialism without realizing that such a self-absorbed and self-consuming way of life is destined to collapse.

Make no mistake: the ultimate disintegration of the New American Landscape is endemic to its character and design. Its promise of perfection in goods and services and the perfectibility of the personalities of its inhabitants is false. Being a false promise, it will only engender a moral hunger within the New Man for that which is genuine, meaningful, and transcendent. Meanwhile, the moral inadequacy, cultural deficiency, and debilitating illiteracy exemplified by the sensibilities of the New Man portend an individual and collective mentality unable to function at the level of complexity and specificity a post-industrial consumer economy requires.

There is an inverse proportion between the amount of graffiti that we see on the walls of our schools and the inability of our youth to read the label of a cereal box. A technical manual on the shop floor, not to mention a college-level text, presents an even greater, if not impossible, challenge. Given the New Man's decreasing academic and technical ability, his value as an economic producer in the brave new global economy becomes increasingly problematic.

How much time remains? How much degradation must we witness and endure on the New American Landscape before fundamental social needs mandate the return, if not of public man, then of communal values? Far too many years of further aesthetic and moral degeneration will transpire before the end of the synthetic environment unfolds. Nevertheless, the very certainty of the inevitable future breakdown of Egotopian hegemony should motivate the critics of Egotopia to consciously prepare for and hasten that eventuality.

Any opportunity to resurrect and reconstruct the physical landscape will be dependent on resurrecting and reconstructing the mental and emotional landscape of the New Man himself. Such a task may not be as hopeless as it may seem. Let us not forget that the moral and intellectual bankruptcy of the New American Landscape is deeply rooted in our contemporary day-to-day experience understanding the depravity of which provides mitigating and corrective direction.

I am reminded of T. S. Eliot's concern about the well-fed mob, who, without the succor of even an oppressive and sometimes insensitive Christianity, to his mind was dangerous and threatening to essential order. Eliot was not referring to civil disorder, though his use of the word mob might suggest so. Eliot was more concerned with an emerging disorder of certitude, an uncertainty of identity, an erosion of the sense of self that is defined within, not apart from, a broader meaningful context. He longed for the certainty that comes from living within the constraints and boundaries of a real community—for Eliot, a Christian community. Such certitude and sense of place, for both the individual and society, Eliot believed to be essential. He saw these stabilizing forces as dependent on the intellectual wisdom and emotional faith made possible only by the nurturing wellsprings of traditional religion as mediated by an established church.

In such a period as the ascension of the New American

Landscape, we can perhaps afford to have a generous and admittedly nostalgic view of the real and imagined benefits of traditional religiosity. Eliot, however, was an American-born Anglophile who would have been more at home in the nineteenth century than in our own. I am more concerned with the inner deprivation suffered by Eliot's mob, for it is a deprivation suffered by children of affluence who have grown up within the great suburban transformation.

How fundamentally uncertain we are, uncertain about our moral bearing, our identity in the universe. Many of us may be well educated, well employed, well paid, and well married. Yet, in spite of our achievements, and in spite of the obligatory material acquisitions that are our birthright, is it not curious that our sense of well-being is so fragile? In comparison to men and women of only twenty-five years ago, many individuals today are like leaves floating on a stream carried by the current to and fro without benefit of normative standards that transcend silly vanities and the fancies of the moment. Certainly it is not romantic nostalgia that informs us of a greater moral certitude and ethical character in even recent past generations. In comparison, our contemporaries create their own morality using the painfully commercial and mostly pathetic inspirations of the self-help literature, the authors of which never cease toiling to improve our spiritual technique.

Egotopia, in both its inward emotional excess and outward manifestation of physical ugliness, is in rapid ascension. The great suburban transformation is in culmination, and we must not be intimidated in the face of its hegemony. At century's end, with the New Man triumphant and with allegedly rational people seriously contemplating the orbiting of billboards in space capable of rivaling the full moon's awesome presence, concerned individuals have choices.

In a very real sense, those who choose to reject the values of the New American Landscape will be perceived as strangers in their own land. As they move amid the moral chaos and aesthetic degradation of the New American Landscape, the New Man will note they do not share his philosophy. Their resistance to the prevailing modalities facilitating self-indulgence will clearly demonstrate that they have refused union with the new order. Those who honor the communal values of public man will encounter the suspicion, the enmity, perhaps even the hostility of the New Man.

Some may choose to hide from that which they find distasteful. Like the very rich, those who oppose the values of the New Man may retreat to the privacy of their own personal environment and attempt to establish a small community modeled in the fashion of the world they hope someday will return. Nevertheless, to keep alive a sense of aesthetics and communal values, it is not to some armed and defended bunker the committed should retreat. As Aristotle said, the virtuous achieve virtue by acting virtuously. In the age of the New Man, the values of civility, community, and aesthetics will live only to whatever extent they shape and guide the public lives and behavior of those who still care about the issues I have identified and discussed.

The residents of the New American Landscape are intellectually vacuous and spiritually bankrupt. For the short run they will sustain themselves and contain their impending frustration and despair with further amusements and novelties, the dissemination of which we as a society so fervently excel. The New Man, however, in his servitude to material pursuits and therapeutic values, is not a hardened ideologue but a creature of simple emotion. In hope of a future restoration of communal values and resurrection of our aesthetic heritage, those who care must offer the New Man that which is genuine, meaningful, and transcendent, a moral alternative to the New American Landscape. Such offering is as much for ourselves as for Eliot's well-fed and well-disciplined mob.

In time, the New American Landscape may yet be sanctified by a resurgence of the communal values that infused and animated the notion of public man. In the end, the sons and daughters of the great suburban transformation will hunger for a way out of the synthetic environment in which they will be little more than prisoners of self-love. Their desire to search for an escape from narcissism and begin the long journey toward the rights and the obligations of genuine community may well become the defining experience of twenty-first-century America.

INDEX

164

Index

165

Index

167

ABOUT THE AUTHOR

John Miller, a Silicon Valley public relations consultant who has seen the social and cultural impact of technology up close and personal, advises clients in fields as diverse as energy conservation, medical instrumentation, and telecommunications. Before founding his own public relations company, Miller was an account executive for the internationally respected Regis McKenna agency, senior public affairs specialist at the Stanford Research Institute, and director of communications for the National Business League. He has also held editorial positions with Cahners and Penton publishing companies. Miller is a founder of Washington, D.C.–based Scenic America, and his writing on public policy and the environment has appeared in the *New York Times,* the *San Francisco Chronicle,* and other publications. He received an undergraduate degree in philosophy from Miami University, Oxford, Ohio, and a graduate degree in mass communications from Florida State University. He lives in the mountains above Los Gatos, California.